PRESENTED TO

BY

DATE

God's Two-Minute Warning

JOHN HAGEE

J. COUNTRYMAN
Nashville, Tennessee

ACKNOWLEDGEMENTS

Grateful acknowledgement is made to the following:

Story on pages 34-35 adapted from *Ride the Wild Horses: The Christian Use of Our Untamed Impulses* by J. Wallace Hamilton © 1952. Published by Fleming H. Revell Company.

Story on page 129 adapted from *Where Now Is Thy God?* by J. Wallace Hamilton © 1969. Published by Fleming H. Revell Company.

Waitley, Denis. 1995. *Empires of the Mind.* Published by Allen and Unwin Co.

Story on pages 109-110 adapted from *Encyclopedia of 7,700 Illustrations: Signs of the Times* by Paul Lee Tan. 1979. Published by Assurance Publishers.

TABLE OF CONTENTS

PREFACE 6

CHAPTER 1
Seize Your Destiny 8

CHAPTER 2
Fear Not 14

CHAPTER 3
Heaven Is Only a
Breath Away 20

CHAPTER 4
Forgive and Be Free 25

CHAPTER 5
Take a Stand for Righteousness . . 31

CHAPTER 6
Choose Your Attitude 38

CHAPTER 7
The Power of Prayer 44

CHAPTER 8
Trust God 49

CHAPTER 9
Be Persistent 55

CHAPTER 10
Save Your Marriage:
Communicate 61

CHAPTER 11
Overcoming Betrayal
and Rejection 70

CHAPTER 12
Live with Confidence 76

CHAPTER 13
Guard Your Freedom 82

CHAPTER 14
Shout for Joy 87

CHAPTER 15
Love in Action 93

CHAPTER 16
Build Wisely 99

CHAPTER 17
Hope for the Troubled Heart 107

CHAPTER 18
Trusting through Trouble 112

CHAPTER 19
Miracles Come in Cans 118

CHAPTER 20
Set an Example 124

CHAPTER 21
Worry Is a Rat 131

PREFACE

Every game played in the National Football League has a two-minute warning. The game stops, and the officials warn the coaches and players that only two minutes remain in the game.

Two minutes. Less time than the average song on the radio. Less time than it takes to heat a cup of coffee in a microwave oven. Two minutes—not much time. A mere 120 clicks left on the clock.

Two minutes left for both teams to take action!

Two minutes that will determine victory or defeat!

Two minutes . . . and then the game will be won . . . or lost.

During these last two minutes, coaches and players pull out all the stops. They may be weary. They may be hurt, banged up, and battered by the opposition. But for two minutes, they all give their very best effort. Everything they have worked for, all the pain and suffering of their brutal profession, culminates within those two minutes.

I believe that we have arrived at the "two-minute warning" on God's clock. Unlike the players in a professional football game, we do not know how much time we have left. What we do with the time remaining will make all the difference in the world . . . and in eternity. Even if we have many years left to live, Christians must strive to be like football players during the last two minutes of the game, pooling our strength and resources, encouraging one another, and working with every trace of energy we can muster to live for Christ. It is vital that we live every day, every moment for Him, seizing the opportunities to represent Jesus to a world that so desperately needs to know Him.

Today is the day of salvation; now is the time to take every thought captive, to tear down any strongholds the enemy of our soul has attempted to build in our lives. We are now "on the clock," and we must make every moment count.

In the pages that follow, you will be challenged, convicted, encouraged, and inspired. Each chapter is meant to be read in approximately two minutes. But although the vignettes are compact, they are powerful, life-changing, and, potentially, *life-saving*! What you do with God's "two-minute warning" may impact your destiny—and the destiny of your loved ones and friends—for all of eternity. We have no time to lose. Now is the time to put forth your finest, to give Jesus everything you have to give. No more excuses, no more wishy-washy levels of commitment. We are heading down the home stretch. We have hell to shun and heaven to gain.

May these pages encourage you to live closer to the Lord Jesus Christ than ever before!

John Hagee
Summer 2000

CHAPTER ONE

GOD'S TWO-MINUTE WARNING

SEIZE YOUR DESTINY

Watch your thoughts, for they become your words.
Choose your words, for they become actions.
Understand your actions, for they become habits.
Study your habits, for they will become your character.
Develop your character, for it becomes your destiny.

You are now determining your destiny. The choices you make today are shaping who you will become.

Though he had great ability, Samson also had a weak character that opened the door for Delilah to deceive him. He allowed Delilah to learn the source of his strength, and the ensuing "bedroom barbershop affair" left Samson powerless and pathetic. His last days were spent grinding grain for his enemies. He was mocked and ridiculed, and his eyes were gouged out because he ignored God's warnings.

David, too, had great ability. He was Israel's poet, prophet, and warrior statesman, but a weakness in his character allowed burning lust to drive him into Bathsheba's arms, producing an illegitimate child. Then he chose to commit cold-blooded murder. But David's two-minute warning came when the prophet Nathan pointed his bony forefinger in the ashamed face of King David and shouted in righteous fury,

"You are the man!" (2 Sam. 12:7). Confronted with his sin, David had two choices—the same choices you and I have when faced with our transgressions—he could repent or flee.

David could have wrapped his royal robes around his body in self-righteous anger and attacked the messenger. He could have reviewed his royal accomplishments and claimed that the blessings of God on Israel were because of his brilliant leadership. He could have . . . but he didn't.

David was no Judas! David was not an emotional coward! David was a man after God's own heart, so he heeded the warning. David fell on his knees before the prophet and sobbed his confession of sin: "Have mercy upon me, O God, according to Your lovingkindness; according to the multitude of Your tender mercies, blot out my transgressions. Wash me thoroughly from my iniquity, and cleanse me from my sin" (Ps. 51:1–5).

YOUR THOUGHTS IMPACT YOUR DESTINY!

Seize your destiny! Make decisions that draw you closer to God, and remember to guard your thoughts. Your every decision is built upon a thought. Saint Paul writes, Bring "every thought into captivity to the obedience of Christ!" (2 Cor. 10:5). Sin does not begin with an action; it begins with a thought.

➤Adultery does not begin at a motel; it begins when your thoughts turn away from your marriage vow made before God.

➤Murder does not begin when you squeeze the trigger; it begins when your thoughts of anger are not brought into obedience before Christ.

➤Divorce does not begin in the judge's chambers; it begins when you entertain thoughts of how good life would be without your spouse.

➤Theft does not begin when you break the window of the jewelry store with a crowbar; it begins when you first imagine how wonderful it would be to have what's not yours.

YOUR SPEECH IMPACTS YOUR DESTINY!

Your thoughts will become your words, and your words will take on powerful implications of their own. Proverbs 18:21 states, "Death and life are in the power of the tongue, and those who love it will eat its fruit."

Notice that there is no middle ground regarding the effects of your speech; your words will lead to either life or death! Wounds inflicted by a sword will soon heal, but wounds inflicted by a toxic tongue cannot be mended apart from the healing power of God's forgiveness.

The teacher of an adult class once gave this assignment to his students: "Go to someone you love and tell them that you love them."

At the beginning of the next class, one of the students told the teacher that he was angry at the assignment because he didn't feel that he could say these words to anyone. He then said,

"But as I began driving home, my conscience started talking. Five years ago, my father and I had a vicious disagreement and never really resolved it. We avoided seeing each other unless we absolutely had to at family gatherings. By the time I got home, I had convinced myself I was going to tell my father I loved him. Just making that decision seemed to lift a heavy load off of my chest.

At 5:30 P.M., I was at my parent's house ringing the doorbell, and as luck would have it, Dad answered the door. I didn't waste any time! I took one step inside the door and said, 'Dad, I just came over to tell you that I love you.'

It was as if a transformation came over my Dad. Before my eyes, his face softened, the wrinkles seemed to disappear, and he began to cry. He reached out and hugged me and said, 'I love you too, son, but I've never been able to say it.'"

Two days after that conversation, the father had a severe heart attack and was hospitalized in critical condition. The son recognized that his thoughts were wrong and took action before it was too late. With his speech, he changed the destiny of his relationship with his father forever.

God's Two-Minute Warning

Your eternal destiny is controlled by your speech. Jesus said, "But I say to you that for every idle word men may speak, they will give account of it in the day of judgment. For by your words you will be justified, and by your words you will be condemned" (Matt. 12:36–37). Look at those two words . . . *justified* or *condemned*. There is no neutral ground. Your thoughts, words, and deeds will determine the destiny of your eternal soul.

Stop and think right now. What have you said in anger to a friend or family member that has poisoned your relationship with that person? Don't hesitate! Go to them today, call them, or write them, but have the courage to say, "I love you!"

CHAPTER TWO

GOD'S TWO-MINUTE WARNING

FEAR NOT

My wife, Diana, and I enjoy going to the movies on our day off. When our five children were small, however, we could barely afford the tickets, let alone popcorn, candy, and sodas for the "Fabulous Five!" In those days, Diana packed sandwiches in her purse, and we ate them during the show.

One day, we walked in the theater with Diana's purse bulging and delicious aromas wafting—her purse smelled like a mobile delicatessen! While Diana stopped to buy drinks, I took the four older children—Tish, Chris, Tina, and Matt—with me into the theater. Diana kept Sandy, our two year old, with her.

With four of the Fabulous Five seated and excitedly awaiting John Wayne and Diana's mobile deli, I sat down, not knowing I was about to experience one of the most terrifying moments of my life—and I've experienced a few scary times over the years!

I once had a demonized man walk down the aisle of my church, point a loaded gun in my face, and scream, "I'm going to kill you on the count of three!" He lied. He started shooting at the count of two . . . and kept squeezing the trigger until every shot was fired. But God's angels miraculously protected me! Amazingly, not a single bullet hit me.

What I was about to experience in that movie theater, however, was far more horrifying. Diana came running down the aisle of the theater, shrieking, and half crying, "Sandy is gone . . . she's missing!"

"What do you mean, she's gone?" I asked, already out of my seat and moving toward the exit. When the well-being of one of my children is in question, I shift into "turbo-drive" in a nanosecond. There was no time to lose.

"Sandy was standing right beside me as I waited in line," cried Diana. "One second she was there, and the next second she was gone! I looked for her all over. She's gone, John. She's gone!" Tears streamed down Diana's face, but this was not the time to console her. *We must find Sandy!* I thought.

Right there and then, God gave me a two-minute warning. I knew instantly, by divine revelation, that someone was trying to kidnap our baby daughter. The iron yoke of fear tried to paralyze my mind to prevent any meaningful action, but my intense love for our daughter overcame the fear. Within three seconds of hearing Diana say, "Sandy's gone," I sprinted the length of the theater aisle, burst into the lobby, and shouted full force, "Lock the doors to this theater! Someone is trying to kidnap my daughter! She is two years old, dressed in a yellow-and-white dress, and has black hair with bangs in the front. Lock the doors NOW!"

I yelled with such force and fury that every person in the theater lobby froze in place. The manager hurriedly approached me and piously recommended that I calm down. I roared at him like a lion, "Be quiet! Lock the doors . . . and lock them now! Do it!" With trembling hands, he did it.

I saw Diana's ashen face. "Go look in the women's bath-room!" I called to her.

"I already looked, and she's not there!" Diana replied tearfully.

"Go look again," I bellowed. "Look in every stall, behind every door!"

As she ran toward the women's restroom, I raced to the men's restroom. No Sandy, not a trace of her! Nothing! Fear had such a strong hold on me that I thought I was going to vomit. I ran back into the lobby, and I saw a scene I will never forget. Diana was standing there with tears streaming down her cheeks . . . and she was clutching Sandy in her arms!

"Where was she?" I asked, weak with relief.

"She was standing on a toilet seat in the ladies' restroom."

Although Sandy was only two years old, she knew her mother was extremely upset. She touched Diana's face with her hands and said, "Don't cry, Mommy. The lady said she wouldn't hurt me if I didn't cry!" Apparently, the woman who had tried to kidnap her had yanked her into the women's rest-room to hide when I started screaming.

Today, Sandy is a premed student at Oral Roberts

University. She has dedicated her life to Christ and is a blessing to our national radio and television audiences—as are two of our other children, Matthew and Tina, who are gifted singers.

I shudder to think what could have happened had I not trampled the spirit of fear and sprinted out into that theater lobby sixteen years ago, screaming like a madman.

God's Two-Minute Warning

Had I allowed fear to hinder me from taking bold and dramatic action, I could have lost my daughter. In what areas of your life have you allowed fear to master you?

➤Do you fear failure? Fear is the father of failure! Remember that God does not manufacture junk, and He does not sponsor flops! God has made no plans for your failure. "For I know the thoughts that I think toward you, says the Lord, thoughts of peace and not of evil, to give you a future and a hope" (Jer. 29:11). God has already planned for your success!

➤Do you fear criticism? Fear of criticism is the kiss of death to achievement. If you're going to lead the band, you must learn when to sound the trumpet and when to keep silent—regardless of what other people say about you.

➤Do you fear other people? In Hebrews, we read, "The Lord is my helper; I will not fear. What can man do to me?" (13:6).

➢Do you fear something from your past? Many people who fear the past go through life running from something that isn't after them. Regardless of what it was, let go of it, and step confidently into the future that God has planned for you.

➢But wait! Do you fear the future? The fear of the future is a waste of the present. Do not fear tomorrow; God is already there!

➢Do you fear death? You have no need to tremble at the thought of leaving this world. Ultimately, death to the believer leads only to eternal life. Jesus said, "And whoever lives and believes in Me shall never die" (John 11:26). Your last breath here is your first breath in eternity.

Remember: Courage is the mastery of fear, not the absence of fear. In the presence of fear, trust God, and take action.

CHAPTER THREE

GOD'S TWO-MINUTE WARNING

HEAVEN IS ONLY A BREATH AWAY

The apostle Paul, one of the most brilliant authors in human history, penned these words about heaven: "Eye has not seen, nor ear heard, nor have entered into the heart of man the things which God has prepared for those who love Him" (1 Cor. 2:9).

Turn your imagination loose for a moment. Let it soar, and dream about a place of such breathtaking beauty that even Paul couldn't describe it. He could only say, *Your wildest dreams can't grasp half the beauty and joy of heaven!*

WHAT IS HEAVEN?

For one thing, heaven is *a place*! It's not a state of mind! It's not an illusion. Jesus promised, "And if I go and prepare a place for you, I will come again and receive you to Myself; that where I am, there you may be also" (John 14:3). Can you imagine the kind of place the King of kings and Lord of lords is preparing for you?

Stephen saw heaven as he was being stoned to death. The Bible records, "But he, being full of the Holy Spirit, gazed into heaven and saw the glory of God, and Jesus standing at the right hand of God, and said, 'Look! I see the heavens opened and the Son of Man standing at the right hand of God!'" (Acts 7:55–56).

➢Heaven is a place of *absolute perfection.* It is four-square, meaning it is perfection personified. Heaven has no sickness, no hospitals, no cancer wards, no surgical rooms, no prisons, no crying, no parting, no suffering—for these former things pass away.

➢Heaven is *a place of reunion.* It is the place where the saints of all ages will be gathered together for an eternal "family reunion." People often ask me, "Pastor, will we know each other in heaven?" My answer is, "Absolutely!"

The Bible says, "And I say to you that many will come from east and west, and sit down with Abraham, Isaac, and Jacob in the kingdom of heaven" (Matt. 8:11). If we will recognize Abraham, Isaac, and Jacob in heaven, won't we recognize each other?

When Jesus rose from the dead, His disciples recognized Him. He encouraged His disciples to touch His supernatural body, saying, "Behold My hands and My feet, that it is I Myself. Handle Me and see, for a spirit does not have flesh and bones as you see I have" (Luke 24:39). You, too, will recognize your family and friends in heaven, just as you recognize them on earth.

➢Heaven is also *a place of promotion!* When men speak of death, they use words such as *farewell, good-bye, the end of life*, and *separation*. But God speaks of death as a precious promotion from this life to eternal life.

King David writes, "Precious in the sight of the Lord is the death of His saints" (Ps. 116:15). Why? Because for the Christian, death is birth into heaven. The process may sometimes be painful, but the end result is so glorious that it staggers the mind of man to grasp it.

WHAT HAPPENS WHEN THE RIGHTEOUS DIE?

In the first moment after your last breath, angels will escort you to heaven, into the presence of God. Jesus implied as much when telling the story of the rich man and Lazarus, the poor beggar. Jesus said, "So it was that the beggar died, and was carried by the angels to Abraham's bosom" (Luke 16:22).

God Himself will meet you at the gates of heaven and wipe any tears from your eyes. Scripture says, ". . . for the Lamb who is in the midst of the throne will shepherd them and lead them to living fountains of waters. And God will wipe away every tear from their eyes" (Rev. 7:17). You'll never have reason to weep again. You'll never have to say good-bye again. You'll never feel physical or emotional pain again; you'll never experience another moment of regret, remorse, or rejection.

You will receive a dazzling white robe of righteousness, without spot or wrinkle. Ephesians 5:27 states, ". . . that He might present her [the bride of Christ] to Himself a glorious church, not having spot or wrinkle or any such thing, but that she should be holy and without blemish." The church is the bride of Christ, and God is preparing us to step into eternity with Him at any moment!

Are you prepared for your "promotion"?

Now is the time to do what God has called you to do. Today is your opportunity to tell someone else about Jesus, to love your neighbor, and to do good in Jesus' name. Remember, the clock is ticking . . . time is almost up.

God's Two-Minute Warning

The best is yet to come!

You need not fear leaving your comfort zone. Men and women cannot discover new oceans unless they have the courage to lose sight of the shore. Now is the time to get ready! Heaven is only a breath away!

CHAPTER FOUR

FORGIVE AND BE FREE

Men with clenched fists cannot shake hands. Too often the trouble with people forgiving and forgetting is that they keep *reminding* us they are forgiving and forgetting! It is essential that we learn how to express true forgiveness, with open hands and open hearts, and with no leftover residue of resentment.

WHAT IS FORGIVENESS?

Forgiveness is the willingness to change your attitude about a strained relationship. Forgiveness is the perfume of a crushed flower on the heel of the one who trampled it. Forgiveness is the key that unlocks the door of resentment and the handcuffs of hate. It provides the grace to change our course in life, preventing collisions that otherwise might prove to be catastrophic.

The following story teaches a great lesson about forgiveness:

> Through the pitch-black night, the captain of a ship saw a light—dead ahead—on a collision course with his vessel. He sent an urgent signal that demanded, "Change course ten degrees east!"
>
> The light signaled back, "Change your course ten degrees west!"

As the light loomed larger, the captain of the ship became angry. He sent another cryptic message: "I'm a navy captain; change your course, mister!"

The reply came back instantly. "I'm a seaman second class. Change your course, sir!"

Furiously, the captain sent a final threatening message: "I'm a battleship, and I'm not changing my course!"

The seaman promptly replied, "I'm a lighthouse. It's your call, sir!"

Forgiveness knows when to seek another route so that you can avoid a foolish, unnecessary, embarrassing, and possibly destructive confrontation. Here are five tips to help you reach forgiveness.

1. **Recognize that forgiveness is an act of your will . . . not your emotions.** If you wait until you *feel* like forgiving, you will live with bitterness in your heart—and that bitterness will destroy you.

A sixteen-year-old girl once asked me one of the most difficult questions I have ever been asked. This brown-eyed beauty looked me in the eyes and spoke with rage seething in every word, "Pastor Hagee, how do you forgive when you can't forget?" Tears streamed down her face as she began to shake with convulsive sobs.

"What is it you can't forget?" I asked.

She didn't answer. Several minutes passed, with neither of us speaking a word. Finally, she blurted through her sobs, "My father raped me repeatedly. My mother knew it and did nothing to stop him!"

Perhaps reading this young woman's plaintive cry causes you to wince. You close your eyes and instantly you are hurled back to a time and place in your life when you were deeply hurt. Maybe you were sexually abused. Maybe you were abandoned by your father or mother or both as a result of a divorce. Maybe you were rejected so totally by your spouse that your self-image was crushed. Whatever the case, forgetting may be out of the question . . . but being healed by the power of forgiveness is possible! You can choose to forgive the person who hurt you because forgiveness is an act of your will.

2. **Recognize that forgiveness heals _you_!** Forgiveness is not necessarily for the person who hurt you—it sets _you_ free. You're not submitting to their brutality, condoning their injustice toward you, or whitewashing the words or deeds of your offender. You are forgiving to bring cleansing to you! Forgive your enemies; it's the only way to liberate your mind and emotions from the toxic poison of that painful memory.

3. **Recognize that forgiveness is your immediate priority!** Jesus said, "Therefore if you bring your gift to the altar, and there remember that your brother has something against you, leave your gift there before the altar, and go your

way. First be reconciled to your brother, and then come and offer your gift" (Matt. 5:23–24).

Forgiveness must take place now! Jesus essentially said, "Stop praying! Forgive the one who has hurt you, and then return to the place of prayer! All the other good things you do in the name of the Lord are worthless until you decide to deal with your own unforgiveness."

4. **Forgive totally!** In Matthew 18:21, the apostle Peter asked Jesus the poignant question, "Lord, how often shall my brother sin against me, and I forgive him? Up to seven times?" Jewish teaching at the time said that if you forgave an offender one time, then you were a good man. If you forgave that same person twice, then you were a holy man. And if you forgave that individual three times, then you were God-like!

No doubt, when Peter asked, "Shall I forgive him up to seven times?" he was fully expecting Christ to praise him for his magnanimous gesture and personal holiness. But Jesus shocked Peter by saying, "I do not say to you, up to seven times, but up to seventy times seven" (Matt. 18:22). That's 490 times!

The message is: Forgive until it becomes a habit. Quit counting offenses! If someone sins against you or offends you in some way, forgive them . . . and keep on forgiving them. You don't have to be a doormat, but you do have to forgive totally, completely, and continually. Forgiveness saves the expense of anger and the high cost of hatred, which waste your physical, emotional, intellectual, and spiritual energy!

5. **Recognize that forgiveness is not optional!** Forgiveness is not something you can do if and when you are "good and ready." God makes it very clear that if you choose *not* to forgive others, He cannot forgive you. Jesus said, "For if you forgive men their trespasses, your heavenly Father will also forgive you. But if you do not forgive men their trespasses, neither will your Father forgive your trespasses" (Matt. 6:14–15).

The New Testament mentions forgiveness sixty-two times; twenty-two of those instances instruct us in the necessity to forgive others. We must forgive now because Christ has already forgiven us. Paul writes in Ephesians, "And be kind to one another, tenderhearted, forgiving one another, even as God in Christ forgave you" (4:32).

God's Two-Minute Warning

The message is clear! Change your course or perish! Your choice determines your future. If you will not forgive someone else, God will not forgive you. If you stubbornly refuse to forgive others, your soul will be lost for all eternity. He who will not forgive others burns the bridge over which he must pass into the gates of heaven.

We have no time to harbor grudges, bitterness, or resentments from the past. We must forgive from the heart and forgive completely. Forgive now! Forgive totally! Forgive and be free!

CHAPTER FIVE

GOD'S TWO-MINUTE WARNING

TAKE A STAND FOR RIGHTEOUSNESS

As the seconds of our lives pass away, do we have time for angry outbursts that might penalize our potential for serving God? The answer is *no*! The Bible says, "Be angry, and do not sin" (Eph. 4:26). It also says, "But whosoever is angry with his brother *without cause* is in danger of judgment . . ." (Matt. 5:22, emphasis mine). The biblical message is clear: At times, anger is good, *if* the cause is godly.

Jesus walked into the temple, the house of prayer, and saw that the place of worship had been prostituted. Sincere Jewish worshipers were being defrauded by money changers in the name of God. No doubt, many good and righteous Jews were as ashamed of the fraudulent practices as Jesus was, but they had long since grown accustomed to the perversion around them.

The outer court churned like the smelly, dirty, noisy marketplace it emulated. The deafening din of merchants hawking their wares, the bleating of the sheep, the cackling of caged birds, the bargaining of gesticulating money changers—the sheer sight and sound of it all must have assaulted the senses.

Into this madness stepped
of God did not come to worship;
with a whip of cords in His hand,
fight against the false values being
house. His eyes blazing with anger,
the money bags off the nearest table
the coins in all directions. He turned
and another, while the religious racke
Terrified that a riot might ensue and wn the wrath of Rome, the Pharisees fled the courtyard before Him. But not before they heard Christ's war cry: "It is written 'My house shall be called a house of prayer,' but you have made it a 'den of thieves'" (Matt. 21:13).

How do we reconcile this scene with the other images of Jesus we see in the New Testament? Did Jesus slip out of character? Did Jesus lose His temper? Did Jesus sin? The answer is *no*! Jesus got angry at the lying, huckstering, and manipulating all done ostensibly in His Father's name.

If we are going to call ourselves Christians, then it is high time that we not only love what Christ loved, but also that we get angry at those things that angered Christ! Anger is not a sinful emotion. Anger is a powerful emotion that God has given each of us to motivate us toward constructive action.

Uncontrolled Anger Will Destroy You

The great composer, Beethoven, is thought to have caused his own deafness by falling into a fit of anger. Physicians tell

trolled anger releases chemical poisons into the
can cause disease and death. Angry people die of
attacks, strokes, or cancer at a much higher rate than
ple who have learned to control their anger. When you
allow yourself to go into an uncontrolled rage, you are not
only committing sin, you are destroying yourself.

Christ is our example in the proper use of anger. When
He cleansed the temple as the Avenger of God, His righteous
anger was for a righteous cause. Yet this same Jesus did not
say a word when He was personally reviled at His Crucifixion,
when He was slapped in the face by Roman soldiers who
mockingly said, "Hail King of the Jews!" That's self-control!
He stood silently before those who planned and perpetrated
His execution.

At the peak of his career, the gifted tenor Roland Hayes—
a black man—stood in Berlin's Beethoven Hall before a hos-
tile crowd of Nazis who had been brainwashed with racial
hatred. How dare this black man believe that he was good
enough to sing at this cultural center for the master race!

As Roland Hayes walked on stage, he was greeted with
a chorus of hisses that grew louder and more vulgar by the
second. For ten minutes he stood before the angry Aryan hate-
mongers in absolute silence. He did not shout back. He did
not walk offstage with drooping shoulders or his head and
eyes lowered to his chest. He stood there in total control of
his emotions until the Nazis, frustrated by their inability to
intimidate Roland Hayes, fell silent.

Roland Hayes then lifted his golden tenor voice and sang until his voice shook Beethoven Hall like thunder. When he finished, the citizens of Berlin were in tears. He overcame their anger with silence and self-control. The Bible says, "He who is slow to anger is better than the mighty, and he who rules his spirit than he who takes a city" (Prov. 16:32).

DO YOU SUFFER FROM MISDIRECTED ANGER?

We probably suffer more from misguided anger than uncontrolled anger. The first Western movies in America were shown to audiences comprised mainly of men who wore six-guns. When the on-screen good guys in the white hats were being beaten up by the bad guys in the black hats, it was not uncommon for the men in the audience to pull their guns and shoot the screen. That's misdirected anger!

I once attended a bull fight in Mexico. I will never go to another because it is a senseless, bloody slaughter in which the bull has no chance. It is, however, a perfect illustration of misdirected anger. The bull is enraged by spears thrown into his neck by a man on a horse. Then the matador enters the ring, and the bull—in blind, misdirected anger—charges the matador's red cape. Again and again, the bull charges, trying to rid himself of the torture and pain he feels. The cape is not the culprit. The bull's real target should be the prissy matador holding the cape. I almost caused a riot in Mexico as I stood and cheered for the bull to "go for the guy holding the cape!"

What are you mad about? Are you attacking the real cause of your anger, or are you attacking everything but that?

ANGER IS POWER WHEN CONSTRUCTIVELY DIRECTED!

Jesus with a whip in His hands—with evil cowering before Him—was as much a Christian as He was while dying on the cross to save the world. Stoics teach that human passion should be bottled up. Buddhists regard passion as an evil to be cast out. But the Bible shows that your emotions are divinely planted. They are heaven's way of mobilizing your forces for the fight. Passionate emotions must not be destroyed; they must be harnessed and put to use, consecrated for the work of the kingdom of God.

Anger is often love's clearest voice! When a mother sees her young child playing in the street, she doesn't mildly request that he consider leaving this "paved thoroughfare of death." She yells loudly, with all her might, "Get out of the street right now!" That's anger—but it is also love, and her love constructively directs her anger.

Similarly, Abraham Lincoln stood on the docks of New Orleans and saw a black woman sold into slavery, snatched away from her loving husband and son. Lincoln was so angry that he dug his fingernails into his hands until they bled. "That's wrong," the tall, slender Lincoln bristled, "and someday, by God's grace, I'll stop slavery."

A rage exploded within Lincoln! Not wild or uncontrolled emotion, but a quiet resolve that drove Abraham

Lincoln through ten humiliating public defeats until he became president of the United States, leading the fight to abolish one of the worst evils in our nation's history.

God's Two-Minute Warning

How can we say we love people, yet we stand by passively while they are wounded or exploited by greedy men and women? How can we allow alcohol and drugs to imprison our youth? How can we allow pornography to mentally rape America? How can we stand in total silence while the Ten Commandments are thrown out of public schools and condoms are brought in? It is time for the church to follow the example of Jesus Christ when He invaded the temple and went to war against the forces of evil.

Some things are worth getting mad about. And the sooner we are willing to take a stand for righteousness, then the better off we will be as a church and as a nation.

CHAPTER SIX

GOD'S TWO-MINUTE WARNING

CHOOSE YOUR ATTITUDE

It is the most powerful message recently introduced to our culture: *If you can control your thoughts, then you can control your world.* This message says that it's not what happens to you that matters; it's how you react to what has happened to you that makes all the difference in your world. Your response to your environment is called *attitude*.

The story of Viktor Frankl, an internationally renowned psychiatrist who endured years of unspeakable horror in Nazi death camps, proves that controlling your thoughts does control your world. The Nazis had killed his family, cut off his hair, took his jewelry and his clothes, and tattooed a number on his arm to replace his name—but they could not take from him his power to choose his response to his environment. He suffered from extreme cold, hunger, and brutal beatings, all in the shadow of the ominous Nazi gas ovens. Frankl, nonetheless, chose to believe that his suffering had meaning.

Thanks to Frankl's "never-give-up attitude" in the face of unspeakable tortures and suffering, he and many of his friends survived the Nazi concentration camp and lived to tell about it. Frankl's book, *Man's Search for Meaning*, describes his experiences in the death camp and the lessons he learned as a result. It has been an encouragement to millions of people.

WHAT IS ATTITUDE?

Your attitude is an inward feeling expressed by your outward behavior. That's why your attitude shows, even when you aren't saying a word. Your actions become a window to your soul. The person who gives "a look that could kill" is not inwardly singing "Oh, happy day!"

Your attitude determines your destiny. It affects your relationship with God, your family, and your friends. Your attitude will determine your success or failure as an employee or employer. Your emotional and physical health will be directly controlled by your attitude.

In his book, *Empires of the Mind*, Denis Waitley shares the true story of a man named Nick, a strong, healthy railroad yardman who got along well with his fellow workers and was consistently reliable on the job. Nick was, however, a chronic pessimist who invariably feared the worst. His attitude was constantly negative.

One summer day, the train crews were told they could quit an hour early in honor of the foreman's birthday. When the other workmen left the site, Nick, the notorious worrier, was accidentally locked in an isolated refrigerated boxcar that was in the yard for repairs.

He panicked! He shouted until his voice went hoarse; he banged on the boxcar door until his fists were bloody. Unfortunately, with all the noises coming from a nearby playground and the roar of the other trains backing in and out of the yard, nobody heard Nick's frantic cries for help.

Aware that he was trapped inside a refrigeration car, Nick guessed that the temperature was zero degrees. *If I can't get out,* he thought, *I'll freeze to death!* He found a cardboard box. Shivering uncontrollably, he scrawled a message on the cardboard surface to his wife and family. "So cold, body's getting numb. If I could just go to sleep. These may be my last words."

They were.

The next morning the crew slid open the boxcar's heavy doors and found Nick's body. An autopsy revealed that Nick had frozen to death. But the car's refrigeration unit was inoperative! The temperature inside was about sixty-one degrees, and there was plenty of fresh air. Because Nick *thought* he was doomed, he was. His attitude became a self-fulfilling prophecy.

You are responsible for your attitude!

When I was a child, my mother quoted a poem to me so often that I never forgot it: "Two men looked out prison bars. One saw mud, and the other saw stars." Two men in the same situation chose completely different reactions! A good attitude produces a good result!

Consider the differences between Saint Paul and doubting Thomas. Paul wrote most of the New Testament from a jail cell. He was also beaten and left for dead, whipped with a

41

Roman cat-o'-nine-tails on numerous occasions, bitten by a deadly viper and expected to die, and shipwrecked and betrayed by his brethren on the shore. Yet Paul wrote, "I can do all things through Christ who strengthens me" (Phil. 4:13).

Thomas, on the other hand, had Jesus Christ as his spiritual mentor. Thomas saw the dead raised to life, the blind healed with sight, and the deaf given hearing. Thomas witnessed Jesus walking on water and many other miracles of the Lord. Yet after all he had seen and heard, Thomas still did not believe the resurrection of Christ. He had the audacity to say, "Unless I see in His hands the print of the nails . . . I will not believe" (John 20:25).

Which of these two men are you like?

POOR ATTITUDES REFLECT A POOR SELF-IMAGE!

People who constantly complain, gripe, whine, and practice the "art" of total misery are infected with a poor self-image. They are deeply insecure! They lack confidence in themselves and their ability. They are afraid to make decisions, so they blame other people for everything that goes wrong. They, of course, are never at fault. They have a bully personality because they are scared to death inside.

When people criticize you unjustly, what they are really saying is, "I feel rotten inside. I don't like the real me, so I'll complain about everyone else so no one will look closely enough at me to discover the real me."

The Bible has much to say about our attitude:

➤ Proverbs 23:7: "For as he thinks in his heart, so is he."

➤ Isaiah 26:3: "You will keep him in perfect peace, whose mind is stayed on You."

➤ Romans 12:2: "And do not be conformed to this world, but be transformed by the renewing of your mind."

➤ Philippians 2:5: "Let this mind be in you which was also in Christ Jesus."

➤ 2 Timothy 1:7: "God has not given us a spirit of fear, but of power and of love and of a sound mind."

God's Two-Minute Warning

Attitudes don't have to be permanent! You have the ability to choose between negative or positive, discouraging or encouraging. If your mouth spews out a perpetual stream of negative comments, you are probably suffering from polluted thinking, and you must choose to cleanse yourself of it. You can do that by replacing negative thoughts with positive, godly thoughts.

Remember that you are a child of God, and the royal blood of heaven is flowing in your veins. You have been created a little lower than the angels. You are an heir and joint heir with Jesus Christ. You are loved! You are special! Keep in mind: A man is not finished when he is defeated; he is finished when he quits.

So don't whine . . . it's time to shine!

CHAPTER SEVEN

THE POWER OF PRAYER

Why doesn't God answer my prayer? That's an often-asked question these days, especially in the crucial moments of our lives. If we are to learn the answer, then we need excellent, unimpeded communication with our heavenly "Coach." We need to learn how to pray with power, knowing in confidence that God hears our prayers and will answer according to His will.

The disciples asked Jesus, "Lord, teach us to pray . . ." (Luke 11:1). As devout Jewish men, they had probably prayed many times throughout their lives. But there was something different about the way Jesus prayed; His prayers had a power that intrigued them. He prayed as though He expected an answer—because He did! The disciples' request indicates that there is a right way and a wrong way to pray, and it is important for us to know the difference. Here are ten simple but effective principles that will help you to pray with power.

1. **Pray in Jesus' name.** The Bible says, "And whatever you ask in My name, that I will do, that the Father may be glorified in the Son. If you ask anything in My name, I will do it" (John 14:13–14). To pray in Jesus' name does not mean that you tack His holy name onto your wish list. It means that your prayers are consistent with what Jesus Himself would pray about a particular situation.

2. Pray according to the Word and the will of God.
"Now this is the confidence that we have in Him, that if we ask any thing according to His will, He hears us" (1 John 5:14). The Word and the will of God are synonymous. To pray for anything not promised in the Word of God is a waste of time, but to pray for what we know is God's desire is a surefire winner!

3. "Pray without ceasing" (1 Thess.5:16). Set aside a few minutes for concentrated prayer every day. Be very still, and get quiet before the Lord. Don't worry if you don't receive instant answers. Remember that Daniel prayed for twenty-one days for an answer to his prayer. Finally, an angel of the Lord appeared to Daniel and said, "We heard you praying the first day, but I was intercepted by the prince of Persia" (paraphrase of Dan. 10:13). Can you imagine that? One of Satan's arch-angels tried to prevent the angel of the Lord from bringing the answer to Daniel's prayer. But Daniel won the battle on his knees. What Daniel did on earth in prayer determined what happened in the heavenly realms, and eventually the answer came. So don't get discouraged. Pray until you get the answer. This is called "praying through."

4. Pray audibly, using simple, natural words. You don't have to impress God with your vocabulary or your spirituality. Do not feel that you must use religious phrases. Talk to God in your own language. He understands it.

5. Do not spend so much time asking God for things, but, instead, confess that God's blessings are being poured

out upon you. For most of your prayer, give thanks to God for the answer that you know, in faith, is coming.

6. **Practice the attitude of putting everything in God's hands.** Ask for the faith to do your best and to leave the results in the hands of a loving God. The Bible says, "Casting all your care upon Him, for He cares for you" (1 Pet. 5:7).

7. **Pray for people you dislike or who have mistreated you.** Resentment blocks spiritual power because it separates us from God.

8. **Practice the presence of God.** You must put yourself in an atmosphere that allows you to focus on Him. The importance of experiencing God's presence cannot be overemphasized. The Bible says, ". . . for in Him we live and move and have our being" (Acts 17:28). After he rediscovered God, Tolstoy expressed this fact in an unforgettable phrase: "To know God is to live."

Isaiah 30:15 says, "In quietness and confidence shall be your strength." Take the phone off the hook, turn the television off, and sit in a chair until you are totally relaxed. Repeat Isaiah 30:15 aloud several times. Picture God standing beside you. Say aloud, "Lord, I receive your presence." Continue saying it until you feel the spiritual power of the living God.

9. **Agree with another believer for the answer to your prayer.** Find another believer and ask that person to join you in prayer for God's answer. The Bible says, "Again I say to

you that if two of you agree on earth concerning anything that they shall ask, it will be done for them by My Father in heaven. For where two or three are gathered together in My name, there I am in the midst of them" (Matt. 18:19–20).

10. **Pray in faith, believing.** Many people say, "Pastor Hagee, my faith is weak." When I hear that statement, I remind them that it doesn't take great faith to believe in a God who never fails. The Bible commands, "Have faith in God" (Mark 11:22). The Scripture also says, "If you have faith as a mustard seed, you will say to this mountain, 'Move from here to there,' and it will move; and nothing will be impossible for you" (Matt. 17:20). Believe that God is hearing and answering your prayer, even as you speak it.

God's Two-Minute Warning

God's Word makes it very clear: prayerlessness is sin. Samuel said, ". . . far be it from me that I should sin against the Lord in ceasing to pray for you" (1 Sam. 12:23). At pivotal moments in your life, prayer should be your first choice, not your last chance. Remember, as powerful as God is, He does not answer prayer until you pray.

CHAPTER EIGHT

GOD'S TWO-MINUTE WARNING

49

TRUST GOD

"Carl has been killed!" the voice on the phone cried to me.

As a pastor of seventeen thousand people, I know full well that every time my telephone rings, I may hear of another tragedy that has struck someone in our congregation. The day I picked up the phone and heard the heartbreaking news of Carl's death is a day that I will never forget. It was a horrible accident that brought unspeakable heartache.

Carl was nine years old and one of the happiest children I have ever known. I had visited his home just a few days before the accident. When I arrived, Carl came running out the door, down the sidewalk, and did a full-straddle split in front of me, as if he was saying, "Wouldn't you like to have a little boy like me?" Little did I know, that was the last time I would ever see Carl alive.

His parents had moved out to the country, where they found room for horses and dogs and countless friends. They were thrilled with their new life, enjoyed rural living, and seemed as happy as could be.

One day, Carl's mother was cutting some tall grass with a tractor, pulling a corn shredder that cut an eight-foot swath. Carl was sitting beside his mother on the wheel housing of the tractor. Suddenly, the tractor hit a deep hole. Carl was thrown off and fell under the shredder. He was killed instantly.

As a pastor, I have never been more devastated by a hardship in our congregation. I look forward to the day when I will see Carl in heaven, a grown man, in the perfection of God, with a new body.

By God's grace and with the help of loving friends and family members, Carl's mother and father recovered from this tragedy, and now, thirty years later, they continue to serve the Lord.

At such difficult times, many people face the nagging question, *Why, God?* Why do bad things happen to good people? It's a question that may never be answered this side of eternity, but there are three points to consider as we seek understanding today: God's plan, our choices, and our ignorance.

GOD HAS A LONG-RANGE PLAN

As difficult as it may be to understand, some tragedies reflect the long-range plan of God. We know that God causes all things to work together for good to those who love Him and are called according to His purpose (Rom. 8:28). We must remember that He has a redemptive purpose for our pain and suffering.

It is not possible for the finite mind of a man to know the infinite mind of God. The Bible says, "For as the heavens are higher than the earth, so are my ways higher than your ways, and my thoughts than your thoughts" (Isa. 55:9). The Crucifixion looked like a great tragedy. The blood-soaked body of Jesus, the promised Messiah, hung on a Roman cross—a portrait of shame and defeat. The disciples had scattered in terror. Those who remained near the cross could only look on in abject horror. It was not possible for Mary, the mother of Jesus, to understand the full meaning of the cross. God's long-range plan that had begun in the Book of Genesis was completed when Jesus said, "It is finished!"

Many things happen in our lives for which we have no answer. No words of explanation can comfort our heart. Sometimes God does not make sense to us. In those times, we must trust the will of a sovereign God and know that He is too loving to be unkind and too wise to make a mistake. Someday, we may understand. In the meantime, we must continue to trust and to believe that although the pain we feel is real, it is temporary.

OUR CHOICES HAVE CONSEQUENCES

Some people blame God when a crisis strikes them—even when, in fact, the problem is frequently the consequence of their poor choices. A big, burly man once sat in my office with his left arm cut off at the elbow. He blamed God for this career-ending injury that happened in a one-man car crash. He had been the driver of the car, and he was drunk at the time of the accident.

He screamed at me as he pointed to his stub, "Look what God did to me!"

I must confess that I was not in the mood to give him the "Harvard Temperament Test." Nor was I willing to listen to him insult our God. Instead, I looked him straight in the eyes and said, "Your stupid choices caused your injury. You chose to get drunk. You chose to drive after you got drunk. You drove the car into the tree, and as a result, your arm was cut off. Quit blaming God. You are living with the consequences of the choices you made."

The man didn't like what I told him, but for the first time, he was forced to face the truth: His tragedy was his own fault.

IGNORANCE IS DANGEROUS

Tragedy is often caused by our lack of knowledge. When President McKinley was shot, he was attended by two physicians, Drs. Weiss and Bliss. Since x-rays had not yet been invented, the doctors could only make an educated guess concerning the exact location of the bullet in the president's body. They followed Dr. Bliss's diagnosis in treating the president, but Bliss was wrong. The president of the United States died as a result. The newspaper headlines screamed the next day: "Ignorance Is Bliss!"

Remember that:

➢ Ignorance can kill you—or someone you love!

➤Ignorance can prevent a cure for cancer or heart disease.

➤Ignorance of God's existence and His power prevents millions from knowing Him.

The last prayer that Jesus uttered was for forgiveness of our ignorance. He looked at His murderers standing around the cross and said, "Father, forgive them, for they do not know what they do" (Luke 23:34).

The recipe for perpetual ignorance is to be satisfied with your opinions and content with your knowledge. Ignorance commonly denounces what it does not understand. It is no wonder, then, that the darkest ignorance is man's ignorance of God.

God's Two-Minute Warning

Solomon wrote, "You are snared by the words of your mouth; you are taken by the words of your mouth" (Prov. 6:2). Words have life! Words have power! When tragedy strikes, you can get bitter or you can get *better*. It's up to you. If you allow your thoughts and your speech to be saturated with resentment, then you will self-destruct. Keep trusting, keep praying, and keep believing, even when you don't understand why you must endure such hardships. The day will soon be here when we will see Jesus face-to-face.

CHAPTER NINE

BE PERSISTENT

Jesus told the story of a man whose friend came for an unexpected visit. The man was unprepared and had no food to offer his friend.

The story has a touch of comedy and a touch of tragedy. The host could not be faulted; after all, he didn't know the visitor was coming. Nor was the visitor to be faulted; there was no phone to call ahead, no postal service by which to send a note to let the host know of his visit. But in the Middle East, hospitality was an absolute must. The host could not send his guest to bed without supper; it would've been a terrible breach of etiquette. *What can I do?* the host must have pondered. Finally, he got an idea. *I have a neighbor*, he thought. *I will go to him and ask him for bread.*

Even though it was nearing midnight, he hurried into the darkness and approached his neighbor's door. He beat on the door repeatedly, fully aware that everyone inside was probably asleep. Nonetheless, he shouted loudly, "Friend! Wake up! Please, my friend, come. Lend me three loaves of bread."

An angry, masculine voice from inside the house shouted, "Do not trouble me. The door is shut, and my children are with me in bed. I cannot rise up and give to you."

Most people would have quit right there! Persistence, however, is the power that prevails.

The man pounded on the door again—this time louder than before—and shouted, "I must have three loaves of bread."

The angry voice inside the house retorted, "You have come too late. Be quiet. You are going to wake up my children. Worse yet, you will wake up my wife, and she will nag me the rest of the night. Leave me alone!"

But persistence prevailed!

The man pounded on the door again . . . louder . . . longer . . . shouting thunderously, "I need three loaves of bread!" At last he heard the sound of bare feet on the floor. Then the door was unbarred, and three loaves of bread were thrust into his hands. He heaved a sigh of relief and went home to feed the friend who had come at midnight.

It is an odd story to those of us steeped in Western culture, but Jesus' listeners must have smiled approvingly as He told of the man's persistence. The Bible is full of illustrations that encourage persistence on the part of God's people!

➤After forty years in exile, Moses returned to Egypt to face Pharaoh and shout, "Let my people go!" God called Moses to return to the place of his worst failure, the place where he had killed an Egyptian and had been forced into exile. Yet Moses obeyed. He went before Pharaoh repeatedly, and eventually, Moses' persistence paid off.

➤ While most of society around him scoffed and laughed at him, Noah worked on the ark for 120 years and persisted until it was finished.

➤ Nehemiah rebuilt the walls of Jerusalem, even while powerful men organized a massive slander campaign to destroy his public credibility. They mocked his work by saying, "If a fox runs on that wall, it will fall down." When their mocking didn't stop him, they attacked his credibility, saying, "You are building a kingdom for yourself." When that failed, they tried to stop him from building the wall by threatening an attack on his life. In response, Nehemiah passed out swords to his workers and set up a watch. They continued building until the wall was completed.

➤ Jacob wrestled with the angel of the Lord until day-break, saying, "I will not let you go except you bless me." His persistence elicited a blessing. The angel renamed him "Prince of God" for his effort.

➤ Daniel prayed twenty-one days for God's answer for the nation of Israel.

➤ When the Day of Pentecost fully came, 120 people received the infilling of the Holy Spirit after ten days of persistent prayer.

➤ Jesus, too, was persistent! The Bible says in Hebrews 12:2, "Looking unto Jesus the author and finisher of our faith; who for the joy that was set before him endured the cross." Notice that He didn't enjoy the cross; He *endured* it. We are free from the penalty of sin because of the persistence of Jesus Christ at Calvary.

Persistence prevails!

Persistence is a fire in your soul. It is the steel in your backbone that will carry you through ridicule, rejection, and reversal.

Persistence cannot be a half-hearted or lukewarm commitment. It's bold! It's daring! It's fearless! When others walk away without bread, persistence keeps pounding on the door at midnight, shouting fearlessly, "Give me three loaves of bread!"

Persistence does not hesitate. It does not look back over its shoulder at yesterday's mistakes. It is not manipulated by the lie that says, "I must have everyone's approval to succeed." Persistence drove Abraham Lincoln to continue through eleven political defeats, an emotional breakdown, and deep depression, so that when he ran for office the twelfth time, he was elected president of the United States. Persistence prevails!

Persistence does not play the role of the victim. The victim says, "My unhappiness is my parent's fault, my spouse's fault, my boss's fault, my teacher's fault." Persistence is a divine fire that burns in your bones and can't be put out.

God's Two-Minute Warning

The very worst of men are those who begin something but give up before it is completed! Jesus said, "No one, having put his hand to the plow, and looking back, is fit for the kingdom of God" (Luke 9:62).

Judas Iscariot began as a disciple of Jesus Christ, but He betrayed our Lord with a kiss and hanged himself. He began well and gave up. He lacked persistence.

Adolph Hitler attended a Catholic school and expressed a desire to become a priest. He began well, but then gave in to the demon spirits that birthed World War II and the Holocaust.

Joseph Stalin attended a seminary, intending to be a healing force in Russia, but he gave up on God and led the Communist Revolution that murdered thirty million Russians. He began well, and then gave up and became the worst of men.

What assignment has God given you? Are you thinking about giving up? Remember, the Bible says, "But he who endures to the end shall be saved" (Matt. 10:22).

Sure, it's tough to live for Jesus nowadays, but this is no time to throw in the towel. This is the time to pull out all the stops, to serve our Savior, and to live for God like there's no tomorrow because persistence wins the reward!

CHAPTER TEN

GOD'S TWO MINUTE WARNING

SAVE YOUR MARRIAGE: COMMUNICATE

Have you ever been misunderstood because of poor communication? Husband, have you ever told your wife something as clearly as you could speak it, and she got it wrong . . . *all wrong?* Wife, how many times have you told your husband something in perfect English, yet he got it wrong . . . *all wrong?* Welcome to communication in marriage! The following story provides a humorous look into this essential ingredient.

A woman went to her attorney to file for divorce. The attorney asked the woman, "Do you have grounds?"

The woman responded, "Yes, about two acres."

The attorney tried again. "Do you have a grudge?" he asked.

She said, "No, we have a carport."

The frustrated attorney then inquired, "Does he beat you up?"

The woman replied, "No, I let him sleep."

The attorney threw his arms into the air and shouted, "Lady, what's your problem?"

"I don't know," she responded. "My husband and I can't seem to communicate."

Unfortunately, that fictitious account may not be too far from the truth for many married couples who are unable or unwilling to communicate.

WHAT IS COMMUNICATION ANYWAY?

Communication is an exchange of feelings or information. It takes two people to communicate, one person sending signals and the other receiving them. Couples, intimidation through temper tantrums is not communication. Husband, yelling at your wife is not communication. Wife, routinely turning on the waterworks to control your husband is not communication. Modern technology has developed communication systems by which we can talk to astronauts who are walking on the moon, yet often husbands can't talk to their wives or children who are seated across the breakfast table from them.

Communication, however, is crucial if we are to make every moment with our loved ones count. We must learn how to express ourselves and how to truly hear what others are saying to us if we are going to defend ourselves against Satanic attacks, tear down the enemy's strongholds, and win the victory.

Communication in marriage means giving your partner the freedom to disagree with you, without either of you flying into a rage or pouting for a week. Communication occurs when you and your spouse can honestly tell each other who you are—all without starting World War III.

Every day, the devil wages an all-out war against godly marriages. We must not allow the enemy to drive a wedge between our ranks. We must keep the lines of communication open. To do so, we need to understand that there are five levels of communication in marriage.

Level five is cliché conversation, which is the poorest level of communication. On this level, we talk in pretense and hide behind emotional masks. We refuse to reveal our true feelings. It may begin with someone asking, "How are you?" Then the response is an automatic and predictable, "Fine!" You may have a 104-degree fever, and be on the brink of convulsions, with blood running out the corner of your mouth, but your answer is, "Fine!" Why? You're just talking; you are not attempting to communicate.

Level four involves reporting facts about other people. On this level, we report the activity of others, which, if we are not careful, can easily degenerate into what the Bible calls "gossip." As Christians we should let four rules govern our conversation. Before you open your mouth to speak about anything or anyone, ask yourself:

1. Is it true?
2. Is it necessary?
3. Are my motives pure in telling it?
4. Will others benefit from my telling it?

If you can't answer all four of these questions affirmatively, then remain silent because silence cannot be misinterpreted.

In *level three,* we share some of our ideas, feelings, and decisions. At this level, we say, "I am willing to give you a peek at the real me, but I will watch your every move carefully. At the first sign of rejection, I will retreat back into my shell. If you raise your eyebrows, narrow your eyes, yawn, look at your watch, or glance at the newspaper or television, then I will retreat to level four or five where little of lasting value will come from our conversation."

In *level two,* we lay down our guard and expose our real feelings and emotions. Jesus asked His disciples, "Who do men say that I am?" Their answers merely reported the facts. Then Jesus pressed in a bit closer and asked His disciples, "Who do you say that I am?" Jesus wanted His disciples to reveal their true feelings and emotions, to express themselves from their hearts.

At this level, our communication goes deeper than superficial conversation. We say, "This is the real me. I am sharing what I feel down deep in my soul. I am revealing what I love, fear, or long for." Communication in marriage must reach and maintain this level without the threat of blowups, pouting, or resentments. If you demand that your spouse agree with you about everything, then you will never reach level two—you will simply be an emotional tyrant.

Level one communication occurs when the symphony of the soul is played—when two human beings interact in absolute honesty, like two violins playing in perfect harmony. All pretense is gone. Fear is gone. There are no snide remarks, and there is no rejection of any kind. At this level, we choose to communicate with transparency and compassion, permitting the other person to respond with total emotional freedom. This sort of communication does not mean that what we say or hear will always be readily accepted.

Jesus communicated with His disciples on a level one basis when He told them that He was going to die. That was not what the disciples wanted to hear, but that was the message Jesus wanted them to know.

Which level describes your marriage?

God's Two-Minute Warning

People who cannot or will not communicate condemn themselves to isolation. In the most important moments of their lives, they dwell alone. In a packed stadium of screaming fans, they will remain unconnected to their most important teammate: their spouse.

Experiencing problems in your marriage is not uncommon, but being unable or unwilling to discuss those problems with your spouse can be dangerous. Communication is the key to an intimate marriage.

We need to remember that Saint Paul commands,

"Husbands, love your wives, just as Christ also loved the church and gave Himself for her . . . So husbands ought to love their own wives as their own bodies; he who loves his wife loves himself" (Eph. 5:25, 28). Love communicates, love expresses itself, and love listens.

Though Paul instructs wives to "submit to your own husbands, as to the Lord" (Eph. 5:22), he explains that this submission is mutual—the husband submits to the need of the wife, and the wife submits to the lead of the husband (see Eph. 5:21). This sort of loving relationship should enhance your levels of communication and intimacy, but this will happen only if you are willing to expose your inner self completely to your partner.

Emotional nakedness requires raw courage. When we reach out with our defenses down, we take a risk, but the benefits of a deeper marriage relationship are worth it! Make your "team" the strongest possible!

Have confidence in yourself as you follow Christ in these exciting days of living out your faith!

JOHN HAGEE

CHAPTER ELEVEN

GOD'S TWO MINUTE WARNING

OVERCOMING BETRAYAL AND REJECTION

Who has not felt the anguish and agony of betrayal? No taste is more bitter than infidelity! And no one knows this better than our Lord Jesus Christ. John 6:64 states, "For Jesus knew from the beginning who they were who did not believe, and who would betray Him." When you're forced to drink from the bitter cup of betrayal, it breaks your heart and leaves an eternal scar that only God can heal.

Our society is saturated with betrayal. Every divorce is born in the womb of betrayal. Every case of child abuse is an act of betrayal. Every lawsuit has its roots in betrayal. Political corruption in Washington, D.C., is a betrayal of the American people. Every act of gossip and talebearing is betrayal. Every Christian who compromises his standards of righteousness for the world, the flesh, or the devil has betrayed the Son of God. He is guilty of treason in the courts of heaven.

History tells the story of Julius Caesar, the powerful emperor who brought Rome to the pinnacle of its majestic power. Rome had conquered its external enemies, and the empire was at peace—but Rome's troubles festered from within. The constant feuding of military men who were vying for positions of power threatened the stability of the government.

Julius Caesar rose to power, and by 45 B.C., he had Rome in his grasp. Not all of Rome, however, was delighted. Caesar was popular with the people, but he was hated by the powerful Roman senate. A conspiracy developed among men who lusted for power themselves, even though they were deeply indebted to Caesar. One of the men of this group was Brutus, Caesar's best friend.

In plotting to murder Caesar, the conspirators agreed that each man would stab the emperor so that the blame could be shared equally. Like vultures, those whom Caesar had once helped converged on him and began to stab him to death.

History records that Caesar fought fiercely against his attackers until he saw the face of Brutus. When he saw the dagger in the hand of his dearest friend, he stopped fighting. Betrayal destroyed his will to fight and robbed his will to live. When Brutus plunged the dagger into the bleeding body of his friend, Julius Caesar had "died" already from the betrayal.

Our Savior experienced the pain of betrayal. Jesus of Nazareth gathered His twelve disciples into the Upper Room for their last supper together. Following the meal, Judas, the betrayer, slipped into the darkness to sell the Son of God for thirty pieces of silver.

Saint Paul was beaten by a Roman cat-o'-nine-tails until the blood ran down his back in streams. But Paul's deepest scars did not come from the scourge of the Romans; they came from the betrayal of fellow believers. Concerning one of his former coworkers who had abandoned him, Paul writes, "Demas has forsaken me, having loved this present world" (2 Tim. 4:10).

Sooner or later, you will be betrayed by a dear friend, or by someone in your inner circle whom you trust without question. The dagger of betrayal will pierce your heart, and the agony in your soul may make death appear sweet.

Jesus warned us in advance that in the last days, even some of our closest relationships may be compromised by betrayal (see Matt. 24:10; Mark 13:12). Don't be discouraged. Don't be swayed from the path of righteousness. Don't grow weary in your walk with the Lord. These things must come to pass before the end. Remember, in your hour of betrayal, when truth seems assassinated by lying lips, when justice is delayed and lies are accepted as truth, God's delays are not God's denials. Your heavenly Father will never betray His children. The God we serve cannot fail to be true to His Word.

Remember how Jesus responded to rejection and betrayal. On the cross, He prayed, "Father, forgive them, for they do not know what they do" (Luke 23:34). Amazing, isn't it? He was dying from wounds inflicted by His oppressors, yet He was concerned for *them* . . . not Himself. That is holy self-control. That is love. Conversely, the mark of Satanic control is self-centeredness.

When Jesus was betrayed, He did not withdraw His love and sulk. Divine love does not draw back or turn away. Divine love is willing to expose itself at the cost of embarrassment, shame, and, yes, even betrayal.

You must decide that you will not be controlled by conditions or circumstances. Look at the word *responsibility*. Look again . . . *response-able*. You are able to choose your response to the crises of life. You can get bitter or you can get better. You can curse the darkness or light a candle. When you choose to place your faith in God, you act, and God reacts!

Eleanor Roosevelt said, "No one can hurt you without your consent. They cannot take away your self-respect unless you give it to them." It's not what happens to you that's important; it's your reaction to what happens that will determine your success or failure. No matter who betrays or rejects you, only you can take responsibility for your mental attitude.

RESPONDING TO THE PAIN

So, how do you respond to betrayal and the rejection that breeds it? When you sense rejection coming, do you close the door, which is the carnal thing to do, or do you open up, and trust God to bring good out of it, which is the divine nature? When Judas approached Jesus in the Garden of Gethsemane, Jesus said, "Friend, why have you come?" (Matt. 26:50). Jesus was saying to Judas, "It's not too late." By reminding Judas of their friendship, Jesus was giving Judas an opportunity to turn away from the devious deed he planned to do. Jesus did not reject His friend, even when He knew that Judas was about to betray Him.

All too often, when we are betrayed or rejected, we in turn reject others. The vicious cycle of rejection, including the inability to give love to another person, can only be broken by God's unconditional love. The power to change comes when you find Christ. The Bible says, "We love Him because He first loved us" (1 John 4:19). You have received love; therefore, you can give love. You have the power to overcome betrayal and rejection because He who knew betrayal and rejection *yet continued to love* now gives that same strength to you.

God's Two-Minute Warning

Betrayal and rejection can wound your heart so deeply that only God can help you to forgive your betrayer completely. Jesus forgave Judas. Paul forgave Demas. We must forgive those who have betrayed us as well. Refusing to forgive, for any reason, damns the soul.

The Lord's prayer says, "Forgive us our debts as we forgive our debtors." You don't have to *feel* like forgiving before you can extend forgiveness. You must *decide* to forgive, and then *do* it! Prayerfully speak the words of forgiveness from your heart, and you will be pleasantly surprised at how quickly the pain of rejection and betrayal can be supernaturally healed. Take this step today!

CHAPTER TWELVE

LIVE WITH CONFIDENCE

It's astonishing how few of us genuinely like ourselves. We live never knowing who we are, probably because if we had the chance, many of us would rather be someone else. Madison Avenue has proven that when we are presented with intriguing role models, we will dress like them, drink what they drink, go where they go, and, of course, buy what they are selling. Why? Because we lack confidence in ourselves. We falsely assume that the people in the ads must have much more going for them than we do, so we foolishly attempt to emulate them.

Living *without* confidence assassinates every opportunity that comes to you. It crushes your dreams and hopes. Living *with* confidence, on the other hand, allows you to take advantage of opportunities and, most importantly, live an effective Christian life even when the pressure is on, making the most of every minute.

WHAT IS CONFIDENCE?

The word *confidence* comes from two words: *con*, which means "with," and *faido*, which means "faith." The word, in its essence, means "living with faith." The Bible says, "Without faith it is impossible to please Him" (Heb. 11:6). Faith is the victory that overcomes the world. Faith starts out before you know how it's going to turn out.

Is faith important for successful living? Just try living one day without it. When you see two people talking in the corner, tell yourself, "They're talking about me." When you go to the bank and deposit your money, tell yourself, "They're stealing my money. I'll never see it again." When you go to the doctor and he says you need an operation to save your life, tell yourself, "I'm okay. He just wants my money." When you go to a restaurant, tell yourself, "The food is not going to be good, and I'm sure they are going to overcharge me." Try living without faith in God or other people for just a few days, and you'll be in a rubber room pounding your head against the wall.

By faith, Elijah was transported to heaven in a chariot of fire long before Steven Spielberg and Hollywood created *Close Encounters of the Third Kind*. By faith, Noah built an ark without a Black and Decker power saw, without the approval of the Occupational Safety and Health Administration, or the endorsement of spotted-owl lovers. He loaded the ark with lions, tigers, and snakes, threw on his luggage, and took a forty-day cruise.

By faith, Abraham, when he was one hundred years old, told his ninety-year-old wife, Sarah, "Honey, turn off the television. I've just been to the Wednesday night prayer service, and God has told me we're going to have a baby." The Bible says Sarah laughed. I think her response was one of pure hysteria. That night, God cranked Abraham's dead battery, and sparks flew from Dan to Beersheba! From a womb that was twice dead came Isaac, "the son of laughter."

By faith, Moses refused to be called the son of Pharaoh's daughter so that he might gain the crown that doesn't fade away. Moses lived to be 120 years old and walked to his own funeral.

By faith, the fathers of the church subdued kingdoms, wrought righteousness, and stopped the mouths of lions— Scripture says these were men and women "of whom the world was not worthy" (Heb 11:38).

DO YOU LACK CONFIDENCE?

You know you lack confidence if you're always looking for a reason why you can't attempt a new task. You say things like, "It won't work. I've tried that before and failed." You refuse to act upon solutions to your problems. When success does not come quickly in a given project, you begin to make excuses rather than seek solutions.

You lack confidence if you fear responsibility. You turn down the promotion at work and sentence yourself to life in a rut. When the boss calls, your first reaction is, "What did I do wrong?" rather than, "My raise finally came through!"

You lack confidence if you become insecure when you meet someone new. You twirl your hair, cover your mouth with your hand, and look into space but never into the face of the person to whom you are speaking. Eye contact is painful for you. Shaking hands with you is like grabbing the back end of a dead fish.

We must keep in mind that in life, we win some and we lose some. You will not land every account. Every customer won't buy. Every phone call is not good news. You won't fascinate every person you meet. You won't win every game you play. But when we know the One in whom we believe, and we are confident that He is able to keep that which we have committed to Him until the end of time, we can have a spring in our step—even when things are temporarily not going our way.

How do we maintain confidence?

How do we overcome those frightening moments in life when we feel inferior or intimidated by what lies before us? How do you keep "running the race," especially when Satan comes after you like a roaring lion? How do you "press on" when it seems like the devil's forces are attempting to overwhelm you, trying to get you to retreat from your dream or divine mission and coaxing you to live in fear and uncertainty for the rest of your life?

First, give up every thought about quitting! The Bible says, "But he who endures to the end shall be saved" (Matt. 10:22). It's not who starts the race that wins; it's who finishes. Stopping at third base is no better than striking out. President Calvin Coolidge said, "Nothing in the world can take the place of persistence. Talent will not. Nothing is more common than unsuccessful men with talent. Genius will not. Unrewarded genius is almost a proverb. Education will not. The world is full of educated derelicts. Persistence and determination alone are omnipotent." Too often, we quit jobs, marriages, schools, and churches because we lack confidence—the rock-ribbed, God-given faith—to endure to the end.

Second, stop making excuses. Two kinds of people populate planet Earth—those who make good and those who make excuses. An excuse is the thin skin of fear stretched tightly over a bold-faced lie. If you are in the habit of making excuses, stop it. You are where you are because of who you are. It's time to move forward in confidence!

God's Two-Minute Warning

1 John 5:14 says, "Now this is the confidence that we have in Him, that if we ask anything according to His will, He hears us." We need to recognize that our lack of confidence is, in fact, the refusal to believe that a sovereign God has the ability to protect and guide us. Confidence is not an emotional matter; it is the consequence of a spiritual relationship with a God who cannot fail. Solomon wrote, "For the Lord will be your confidence, and will keep your foot from being caught" (Prov. 3:26). Have confidence in God! Have confidence in your fellow believers! And have confidence in yourself as you follow Christ in these exciting days of living out your faith! Will you trust in the one true "Coach" who perfectly guides us in all things?

CHAPTER THIRTEEN

GOD'S TWO MINUTE WARNING

GUARD YOUR FREEDOM

Mention the word *freedom*, and every American stands tall. Freedom runs in our blood. This is the land of the free and the home of the brave. We have freedom of the press, freedom to bear arms, freedom of public assembly, and freedom of speech.

When I preached behind the Iron Curtain, I asked a generation of Germans who had lived their lives behind that wall, "Are you free?" Their instant response was, "Of course!" It dawned on me that if all you've ever known is captivity, then you'll think you're free even when you are not.

Why do you want to be free? Wanting freedom is, in itself, of no particular virtue. Every bird wants to be free. Every fish wants to be free. Every wild animal will fight you to the death for his freedom. Why do you want freedom? What are you going to do with it?

Freedom can be dangerous. If not properly handled, you could destroy yourself with it. For instance, the prodigal son sought freedom from his father, but it nearly destroyed his life. He left home saying, "Give me," and he returned home saying, "Make me." Fortunately, in between those times, he discovered that freedom is the right to do as you ought, not simply the right to do as you want. He discovered that freedom carries responsibility, and choices have consequences.

Portrait of Freedom

As we watch the clock of history ticking off the seconds, we are forced to face the real facts about our own personal freedom. What does your freedom look like? If you knew that you had less than 120 seconds to live, wouldn't you want true freedom, a real liberty that comes from God? This kind of freedom requires two important conditions.

First, *freedom requires community.* Simply stated, we need each other. Our lives are linked together. I cannot do something that hurts you without hurting me. That's true in every marriage, every church, and every nation. True freedom means we must make sacrifices for each other.

Second, *true freedom requires that you make choices.* Choices have consequences. Every marriage is a result of choice. Sir, don't criticize your wife's faults. Those very faults kept her from choosing a better husband! We must live with the choices we make, so make them carefully.

Every career is a matter of choice. You chose your job, and you need to get excited about it. There is a word for those who are not excited about their job. That word is *unemployed.*

Third, *true freedom never should come at the expense of conscience.* Conscience is that small, inner voice that God has given us to help discern right from wrong in moral, ethical, and spiritual matters. To some people, a clear conscience is nothing more than a poor memory. When a man won't listen to his conscience, it's usually because he doesn't want advice from a stranger. Guard your conscience, and it will help guard your freedom.

Fourth, *you are never free until you voluntarily allow yourself to be mastered by Someone greater than you.* God has never set anyone free to do their own thing. When Moses led the children of Israel out of Egypt, they did not become desert hippies. God immediately gave them the Ten Commandments.

When Jesus preached His first sermon, He said, "I have come to set the captives free" (paraphrase of Luke 4:18). "Free to do what?" we might ask.

Jesus would remind us, "You are not free to do your own thing, but to take up your cross and follow Me." You must be bound to something greater than yourself. The apostle Peter said, "Live as free men, but do not use your freedom as a cover-up for evil; live as servants of God" (1 Pet. 2:16, NIV). With freedom comes a great responsibility! The Bible also says, "If the Son makes you free, you shall be free indeed" (John 8:36). You are not free to do your own thing. You are free to be a servant of God.

God's Two-Minute Warning

Americans are passionately pursuing false freedoms that are destroying this nation. Divorce is freedom from fidelity. Children of absentee parents are scattered like straw in a tornado. They weep in the night, and there's no one to comfort them because Mother and Dad are "free."

The drug culture is freedom from reality. America is spending billions in the war on drugs, but it is a complete failure. Millions of our young people have bodies that are destroyed and minds that are forever crippled. They will never live a productive day as a result of their foolish use of drugs.

As a nation, we are worshiping other gods and calling it "multiculturalism." We have endorsed sodomy and called it "an alternative lifestyle." We have condoned laziness and called it "welfare." We have polluted the air with profanity and pornography and called it "freedom of expression."

Those "freedoms" are nothing more than bondage in disguise. False freedom says we are free enough to break the law of God. But the wise person knows that nobody breaks the law of God; the law of God breaks us when we choose to disobey it. True freedom—the kind Jesus Christ brings—allows us to enjoy the liberty of God's Spirit. We are truly free if we choose to live safely and securely inside the boundaries He has fixed for us, inside the rules He has set for our triumph.

CHAPTER FOURTEEN

GOD'S TWO-MINUTE WARNING

SHOUT FOR JOY

Stress. Worry. Tension. We live in an unhappy world—have you noticed? All you have to do is listen to the "doom jockeys" on the national news, with their endless litany of gloom, despair, and pessimism. America represents 6 percent of the world's population, yet we take 90 percent of the world's tranquilizers. The message? We're uptight!

One lady said, "The only thing holding me together is my hairspray." Another person said, "The only way to wake up with a smile on your face is to go to bed with a coat hanger in your mouth."

The spirit of doom and gloom has invaded the church. There is a saddening lack of old-fashioned, simple-hearted, overflowing, life-changing joy in the church of Jesus Christ. When you look at the countenance of the average American congregation, it looks like a reprint of the Book of Lamentations!

Yet throughout the Bible, God's people are instructed to rejoice. King David said, "Let Your saints shout for joy" (Ps. 132:9). Nehemiah said, "For the joy of the Lord is your strength" (8:10). Solomon wrote, "A merry heart does good, like medicine" (Prov. 17:22). Medical science is now saying that laughter releases endorphins, a substance in the brain that helps the body fight disease and releases healing power. It's nice to see that modern science is catching up to the Bible! God's Word informed us a long time ago that physical healing takes place when we experience joy.

THE POWER OF JOY

While I was on the East Coast speaking at a conference, a very gracious woman from West Virginia approached me. She shared with me one of the most moving testimonies I have ever heard. She told me that her father, a very successful farmer, was diagnosed with terminal cancer. The cancer had grown in his stomach to the point that tumors on his internal organs could be seen through his skin.

His friends came by his home to bid him farewell as he made preparations to die. But then one day, he heard me speak on national television about the power of joy. He ordered a tape of the message, "Being Happy in an Unhappy World," and he listened and laughed. He listened again and laughed again. He listened until he wore out the tape and had to order another one. He put his tape player on automatic reverse and continued listening to the tape, over and over again. He played the tape for all of his friends who visited him.

Amazingly, after several days, his appetite returned. Then to everyone's surprise, the tumors in his stomach started to shrink; the lumps beneath his skin were no longer visible. He went to his doctor, and the physician stated that the cancer was in remission. It's true; the joy of the Lord is your strength!

Jesus Christ gave us three cheers: "Be of good cheer, I have overcome the world" (John 16:33), "Be of good cheer, your sins are forgiven you" (Matt. 9:2), and "Be of good cheer, it is I; do not be afraid" (Matt. 14:27). The gospel message of the New Testament begins with a song and ends with a song. Christianity begins with angels singing over Bethlehem's manger, "Joy to the world, the Lord is come!" It ends in Revelation with the saints singing the song of the redeemed on the sea of glass.

Christianity without joy is Christianity without credibility. Jesus ordained joy in His Sermon on the Mount. It's the Magna Carta of happiness; His audience consisted of Jews living in bitter political oppression from the iron fist of Rome. Similarly, Paul and Silas sang for joy in a jail after they had been beaten until they bled. The fathers of the church sang as they were being led to the stake to be burned alive. The joy of the Lord does not depend on our circumstances.

JOY IS A CHOICE

The apostle Paul said, "Rejoice in the Lord always. Again I will say, rejoice!" (Phil. 4:4). Notice that we can choose to rejoice, no matter what. Or to put it another way, you rejoice by choice. You are as happy as you decide to be.

America's latest fad is called "happy hour." That's where a community of drunks get together and cry on each other's shoulders. The only legitimate happy hour on planet Earth is when God's children get together, for the Word of God says, "In Your presence is fullness of joy" (Ps. 16:11).

Two barriers often block our joy. The first is the attitude that someone else has created your problem. This is playing the role of the victim, which has become one of America's favorite pastimes. Whatever you have become or done, you cannot blame anything on anyone but yourself. No one can take your God-given freedom unless you hand it over to them.

Second, I've heard hundreds of people blame their behavior or situation on their parents. They whine, "My parents didn't love me!" That's good freshman psychology, but it's pathetic theology. The Bible says that when we come to Christ, we become new creatures: "All things have become new" (2 Cor. 5:17). You have a new heart, a new attitude, and a new life. If your parents truly didn't love you, I am sorry, but the good news is that God Almighty loved you enough to give His only begotten Son for your redemption.

Can you have joy in a time of suffering? Yes! Jesus did! The Bible says that He endured the cross for the joy that was set before Him (see Heb. 12:2). Paul did! He sang in the midnight hour in a Roman jail after being beaten.

Whatever trial you're going through, God's joy is available to you if you will receive it by faith. The Bible says, "This is the day the Lord has made; we will rejoice and be glad in it" (Ps. 118:24).

God's Two-Minute Warning

To reject Jesus' joy is to reject Jesus because the Bible says, "In Your presence is fullness of joy" (Ps. 16:11).

91

To allow other people to take your joy is to disobey the Word of God that says, "Your joy no one will take from you" (John 16:22). Moreover, to reject the joy of the Lord is to embrace depression and despair. For an athlete who experiences a career-ending injury, a businessperson whose venture doesn't make it, a student who doesn't make the grade—there is joy. Do not allow your situation, your crisis, or your trial to separate you from the joy of the Lord.

"But I don't *feel* joyful," you might say. That's okay. Remember, joy is a choice. As an act of faith, shout for joy, and the feeling of joy will follow. Seize the moment with joy!

CHAPTER FIFTEEN

LOVE IN ACTION

The word *love* is the most used and most misunderstood word in the human language. That universal word tumbles from our lips randomly and habitually, but what does it mean?

Love is not emotion. A young man once told me that he felt sure he was in love because when his girlfriend entered the room, he couldn't breathe. I told him he had the genesis of asthma . . . not love.

Love is not what you say; love is what you do. A young man was speaking to his fiancé and said, "I love you more than life, my darling. Without you, life has no meaning. I'd crawl across the desert on my hands and knees to see you. I'd swim the oceans to touch you. I'd fight wild tigers with my bare hands to save you."

She asked him, "Will I see you tomorrow night?"

"Yes," he replied, "if it doesn't rain."

Love is more than emotion and words! Jesus didn't say, "I was hungry, and you felt sorry for me. I was naked, and you felt shame for me. I was in prison, and you were embarrassed for me. I was sick, and you were sympathetic with me." He said, "I was hungry, and you didn't feed me. I was naked, and you didn't clothe me. I was in prison, and you didn't come to me. I was sick, and you didn't visit me." In the mind of Christ, love is measured by what you do or what you do not do. Our lives are shaped by those who love us and by those who refuse to love us.

Without love, you are spiritually dead. 1 John 3:14 records, "We know that we have passed from death to life, because we love the brethren. He who does not love his brother abides in death."

The apostle Paul gave us a portrait of love in 1 Corinthians 13: "Though I speak with the tongues of men and of angels, but have not love, I have become sounding brass or a clanging cymbal. And though I have the gift of prophecy, and understand all mysteries and all knowledge, and though I have all faith, so that I could remove mountains, but have not love, I am nothing. . . . And now abide faith, hope, love, these three; but the greatest of these is love."

In those verses, Paul repeatedly says, "Without love, you are nothing." When I was in seminary, struggling financially to stay alive, I went to a junkyard to buy a spare tire. While there, I made the mistake of using the word *junkyard* in the presence of the owner. He looked at me very sternly and responded, "This is no junkyard. Junk is something that has no value and can no longer make a contribution to anyone's life. You are looking at an ocean of opportunity. You are here because something I have can make a positive contribution to your life. This is not junk."

I never forgot his message. Without love, you do not have the ability to make a contribution to anyone's life. The objective of the believer is to become conformed to the image of God. But what is God like? How can He be described? The Bible's most powerful definition of Father God is this: "God is *love*."

Paul said, "Though I speak with the tongues of men and angels, but have not love, I am nothing." Throughout my life, I have studied Latin, Greek, Hebrew, Spanish, and English and have mastered none of them. But even if I could speak fluently in each of those languages, it would make no difference without love. If I spoke every language and every dialect on planet Earth, I might be prone to say I am something special, but Paul says, "Without love, I am nothing."

Paul continues, "If I understand all mysteries . . ." Even if we could solve every dilemma, our efforts would be useless without love. Every week I walk the corridors of San Antonio's hospitals and visit people who will never go home. Their bodies are full of cancer. Cancer is a mystery that brilliant men and women are working day and night to solve. Billions of dollars are being spent to find the cure to this deadly disease. What if I discovered the cure? What if my discovery solved the mystery of every form of cancer on Earth? Certainly, I would win the Pulitzer Prize for Medicine. Reporters from *Time, Newsweek, USA Today,* and television stations would swarm into my front yard, begging me for an interview. In my natural self, I might be prone to say, "I am really something now!" But Paul says, "Without love, I am nothing."

Paul continues by saying, "And have all knowledge . . ." What if I possessed knowledge in the field of chemistry so profound that Linus Pauling would be intimidated? What if I had such a profound mastery of mathematics that I dwarfed the accomplishments of Albert Einstein? What if I mastered political science so completely that Henry Kissinger would hide in a closet when I entered the room? In my natural self, I would say, "Wow! I am something." But Paul says, "Without love, I am nothing."

Love is patient! That means it never gets tired of waiting. Love never gives up. We don't understand a God who is both powerful and patient, but part of the greatness of God is His patience—He is slow to anger. Aren't you glad of that?

Love is kind! Love looks for a way to be constructive. Kindness is the ability to love people more than they deserve. Kindness is a language that the deaf can hear and the blind can see.

Love envies not! A person often criticizes the individual whom he secretly envies. The man who belittles you is trying to cut you down to his size. When you feel yourself turning green with envy, you are ripe for trouble.

Love is humble! Love does not flaunt itself. Love does not boast. Love does not put itself on display. Love makes no parade. Love has no pride. God's love is always willing to forgive and forget at the risk of being embarrassed.

Love does not behave unseemingly, which means love has good manners. Love is unselfish, for "love does not seek its own"; love has self control, for "love is not provoked." Love is not irritable. Love is not fretful or touchy. Love is not quick to take an offense.

God's Two-Minute Warning

To refuse to love other people is to reject the love of God. How can you say that you love God whom you have not seen, and love not your brother whom you have seen? To have a vertical relationship with God, you must have a horizontal relationship with your fellow man. The rejection of the way of love is a rejection of God, but to love unconditionally as He loves is the highest and most noble experience we will know here on Earth!

"Pursue love" today (1 Cor. 14:1)! The people in your life need to know of your love!

CHAPTER SIXTEEN

GOD'S TWO-MINUTE WARNING

BUILD WISELY

Solomon repeatedly extolled the virtues of wisdom when he said:

"Happy is the man who finds wisdom,
And the man who gains understanding;
For her proceeds are better than the profits of silver,
And her gain than fine gold.
She is more precious than rubies,
And all the things you may desire cannot
compare with her.
Length of days is in her right hand,
In her left hand riches and honor.
Her ways are ways of pleasantness,
And all her paths are peace.
She is a tree of life to those who take hold of her,
And happy are all who retain her"
(Prov. 3:13–18).

Wisdom is the compass by which man is to steer across the sea of life. Without wisdom, man is as the wild donkey; he runs here and there wasting his strength and resources, living life in absolute futility.

Wisdom does not waste time responding to its critics. You don't stop the parade to pick up a dime. Wisdom refuses to allow you to major in minor things. Wisdom reminds you that the more you know, the less you fear. Wisdom proclaims that what's right isn't always popular and what's popular is rarely what's right.

American society is being inundated with an emphasis on "individual rights" at the expense of our rights as a people. "I have my rights!" seems to be the answer to every argument, no matter how frivolous. We must learn as a society that when we declare our rights, we cannot forget our responsibilities. Freedom is not the right to do as you want. It's the opportunity to do as you must.

Wisdom reminds us that not getting what you want is often a divine blessing. Billy Graham's wife once said that she was delighted that God didn't answer every prayer in the way that we desire. Had God answered her prayer, she would never have married Billy Graham. Often, the wisdom of God withholds from us the thing we want at the moment so that a greater good may be accomplished in and through our lives in the future.

The voice of wisdom says:

➤The problem that infuriates you the most is often the problem God has assigned you to solve.

➤What you are willing to walk away from determines where God will bring you in life.

➤When you want something you've never had, you must do something you've never done.

➤God never consults your past to determine your future.

A story is told of a wealthy businessman who made a fortune in the home-building business. Near his time for retirement, he told his foreman, who had worked for him for thirty years, to build the most beautiful house he could imagine. The foreman was told to spare no expense because this was to be the last house they would build together before the owner retired.

The foreman was informed that the buyer and his wife were going to Europe for one year. During this time, the foreman would have all the money and resources he needed to build the house. When the buyer and his wife returned, the magnificent house was to be completely finished.

Great! the foreman thought. *This is my chance to make some quick money. I'll use inferior materials and charge high prices on this last project.*

At the end of the year, the owner asked the foreman to show him the beautiful home that represented his finest efforts. The foreman showed the owner the home, which, on the surface, was exceedingly beautiful but, in reality, had been built with inferior materials. The house appeared to be magnificent.

Upon seeing it, the owner handed the foreman the keys and said, "Thank you for your outstanding service to me all these years. This house is your finest effort. I am giving it to you. It is my gift to you. It's yours. Live in it!"

In Proverbs 9:1, Solomon describes wisdom as a house. Indeed, each of us, through wisdom, is building a house called *life* that we will live in, either protected from the storms or exposed to endless peril. God Almighty will force you to live in it. What sort of materials are you using in your house, especially in the areas that the naked eye cannot see? Solomon, the wisest man in the world, said, "Wisdom has built her house, she has hewn out her seven pillars" (Prov. 9:1).

The first pillar of the house that wisdom builds *is the fear of the Lord*. Proverbs 1:7 states, "The fear of the Lord is the beginning of knowledge." We desperately need a fresh understanding of the awe-inspiring, reverential fear of the Lord. America is in a moral free-fall because we have lost our fear of God. The Ten Commandments are ridiculed. The name of God is used in endless vulgarity. Hollywood portrays Christ on the cross as a lust-driven, demonized lunatic who had sexual hallucinations of Mary Magdalene while hanging on the cross at Calvary. If we understood even for a moment Who we will stand before on Judgment Day, then we would once again have a fear of God in this nation.

The second pillar of the house that wisdom builds is *mercy*. Mercy is a disposition of the soul. Mercy projects a forgiving spirit, a heart of compassion, and the mind of Christ toward the suffering or the sinful.

Mercy will be manifested! You may have the money of Rockefeller and not show it, or the musical skill of Beethoven and not reveal it, or the knowledge of Albert Einstein and not expose it, but if you have the mercy of God, it will be manifested. You cannot hide it. Like oil trapped beneath the earth's surface under great pressure that is released by the driller's bit, so mercy explodes in torrents from the hearts of God's children.

Mercy has the ability to feel what another person feels and to see life from someone else's perspective. A story is told of a pastor who was having his shoes shined. He was in a hurry. When he thought it was time for the task to be finished, he looked down only to find his shoes in worse condition than when he first sat down. He started to speak sharply to the little shoe-shine boy, but then he noticed the little fellow's face was wet with tears that were dripping off his cheeks. The boy said, "I'm sorry, sir, but my mother died this morning, and I'm trying to make enough money to put some flowers on her casket." The tears falling on the shoes made it impossible for the boy to shine them. When the pastor knew all, he forgave all. The sharp words in his mind dried up in his throat when he saw life from the boy's perspective.

The third pillar of the house that wisdom builds is _trust_. Solomon said, "Trust in the Lord with all your heart, and lean not on your own understanding; in all your ways acknowledge Him, and He shall direct your paths" (Prov. 3:5). The human race is held together by trust. We put our money in a bank and trust that it will be safe. We go to the doctor and trust that he will competently care for our ailment.

We get on an airplane and trust that the plane is air worthy, that the pilot is capable, and that the plane is, in fact, going to our destination. Every friendship and every marriage is held together by trust. My relationship with God is based on trust.

The **fourth pillar of the house that wisdom builds is _money management._** Solomon said, "Honor the Lord with your possessions, and with the firstfruits of all your increase" (Prov. 3:9). The man who gives nothing to God will live in poverty, but he who gives generously will be blessed.

The **fifth pillar of the house that wisdom builds is _happiness._** Solomon said, "Happy is the man who finds wisdom" (Prov. 3:13). Are you happy? Or have you lost the ability to laugh? Happiness is a choice that you make every day.

The **sixth pillar of the house that wisdom builds is _confidence._** Solomon said, "For the Lord will be your confidence" (Prov. 3:26).

The **seventh pillar of the house that wisdom builds is _grace._** Solomon said that wisdom will be "grace to your neck" (Prov. 3:22). When you give up what you deserve, God will give you more than you dreamed. Grace gives you the power to look beyond another's faults to see their potential in God.

God's Two-Minute Warning

To reject the wisdom of God is to invite the judgment of God. Solomon declares,

"Wisdom calls aloud outside . . . because I have called and you refused . . . because you disdained all my counsel, and would have none of my rebuke . . . I will mock when your terror comes, when your terror comes like a storm . . . when distress and anguish come upon you. Then they will call upon me, but I will not answer; they will seek me diligently, but they will not find me. Because they hated knowledge and did not choose the fear of the Lord" (Prov. 1:20–29).

Without the instruction of their coach, even the best athletes cannot play to their top potential. Likewise, as players on the field of life, we need wisdom from God to make successful decisions that will honor Him.

CHAPTER SEVENTEEN

GOD'S TWO-MINUTE WARNING

HOPE FOR THE TROUBLED HEART

Sooner or later, each of us experiences pain and frustration in the troubled times in which we live. We feel stress from an economic downturn or a major health crisis. We may also feel desperation in a marriage crisis or in other personal relationships. We may suddenly, and unexplainably, experience a tragedy that strikes like lightning out of a clear, blue sky. Things go wrong, people disappoint us, and our problems mount.

We want to improve our lives, but it seems we're in a state of constant crisis. How can I face failure and disillusionment realistically and still be optimistic? How can I learn to have faith again in people who have failed me? Where can I find hope in the dark days of deep depression, or those long, lonely nights permeated by pain? Where can I find strength for the storms of life that I see approaching on the horizon?

The Bible says, "Lay hold of the hope set before us. This hope we have as an anchor of the soul both sure and steadfast" (Heb. 6:18–19). Hope is the anchor of the soul that will hold you through the storms of life. Hope is a periscope that enables us to see over our present problems to future possibilities.

Hope is a powerful medicine for despair and depression.

David says, "Why are you cast down, O my soul? Why are you disquieted within me? Hope in God, for I shall yet praise Him for the help of His countenance" (Ps. 42:5). Similarly, Saint Paul says we should be "rejoicing in hope, patient in tribulation, continuing steadfastly in prayer" (Rom. 12:12).

Our greatest possession in life is the hope we have in God. Hope is to dreams what baking powder is to biscuits. A hopeful person is someone who takes along a camera and the tartar sauce when he goes fishing for Moby Dick! The most significant factor between success and failure, victory and defeat, and often even life and death is hope.

Hope is a cactus and not a cushion. It makes you jump up and do something to solve the problem. Hope is putting faith to work, when doubting would be easier. Hope gives you the ability to be happy with what you have while working for what you want.

Never deprive someone of hope. It might be all they have. It may be what keeps them going when it is easier just to give up and die. During the dark days of World War II, an American submarine sank off the coast of New England. Still alive as the submarine settled on the bottom of the ocean, the sailors restricted their every movement to keep from burning up precious oxygen. American rescue ships raced to the scene, divers probed the dark, murky waters, but their efforts were futile. Finally, just as the search was about to be called off, the rescuers' equipment picked up a sound emanating from the deep. Using a wrench, a sailor in the submarine was beating out a message in Morse code: "Is there any hope?" The message inspired the rescue crews to try again, and the sailors were saved. That's what hope can do!

Hebrews 11:1 states, "Now faith is the substance of things hoped for, the evidence of things not seen." Hope that is founded on the Word of God is not mere sentimentality. It's as solid as the Rock of Ages. Hope is faith putting out its hand in the dark with absolute confidence. When the storms of life are raging, when winds and waves pound your soul, when tragedy strikes and darkness surrounds you, when failure seizes you by the throat, lay hold of the hope that is the anchor of your soul.

In pagan cultures, hope is not considered a virtue; it is an evil to be shunned. In Buddhism, for example, hope is regarded as a deceiver and a betrayer. The same was true of the Mediterranean world when Jesus Christ began His earthly ministry. The Greeks and the Romans did not tempt themselves with hope. They wanted nothing to do with what they considered to be foolish delusions.

Then came Jesus of Nazareth, standing before the multitudes on the shores of the Sea of Galilee, saying, "But seek first the kingdom of God and His righteousness, and all these things shall be added to you" (Matt. 6:33). In His message, people found hope for a better life. When the message of God's Word is delivered and obeyed, a nation's standard of living rises, and people are inspired to hope. Where the message of God's Word has been rejected, a nation and its people live in poverty, disease, and utter hopelessness.

Hope will motivate you to accomplish the impossible. The story of Abraham demonstrates the power of God-given hope to do the impossible. Abraham was one hundred years old, and his wife, Sarah, was ninety. You don't need to be a doctor to know that having a baby at their ages was utterly impossible. Yet Paul writes in Romans 4:18 that Abraham "who, contrary to hope, in hope believed so that he became the father of many nations, according to what was spoken, 'So shall your descendants be.'"

Remember, you can never rise any higher than the hope that rises in your heart. Hope in God.

God's Two-Minute Warning

Solomon said, "Hope deferred makes the heart sick" (Prov. 13:12). To reject hope is to embrace despair and desperation. Indeed, the rejection of hope is the rejection of God, for God is called "the God of all hope."

No matter what our calling, hope is available in our daily decisions. There is hope for the troubled heart and hope for every crisis known to man. Paul says in Romans 8:24, ". . . for we were saved in this hope." Hope is not *something*; hope is *Someone*! Jesus Christ is called the Hope of glory. Place your hope in Him.

CHAPTER EIGHTEEN

TRUSTING THROUGH TROUBLE

Going out to meet trouble is one of life's shortest trips. Yet trouble is often the gateway to discovering the power and presence of God. After all, how can you know God as Healer without being sick? How can you know God as your Provider without feeling the pinch of need? How can you know God as a Friend that sticks closer than a brother without feeling lonely or rejected? How can you know God as your Deliverer unless you have lived in the chains of captivity, bound by weaknesses and habits that have enslaved you? When trouble comes—and you can be sure that it will—look at it as an opportunity for God to work His wonders in your life.

Imagine that you are a king or queen with unlimited wealth. One day, you see a ragged, hungry child begging on the streets. You say to the child, "Here is a royal decree. Call on me tomorrow at the palace, and I will meet your every need." When the child came to the palace the next day, full of hope and expectation, would you not help? Of course you would!

Now, consider this: Jesus Christ, the King of glory, has written a royal decree to His children. The decree is the Word of God, in which the King promises, "Call upon Me in the day of trouble; I will deliver you" (Ps. 50:15) and "Ask, and it will be given to you" (Luke 11:9). No matter how tight your budget, or what difficulty you face, you can trust the Lord to provide everything you need! He will not deliver you from trouble; He will deliver you *through* your trouble.

No one ever gets beyond the reach of trouble. No wall is high enough, and no door is strong enough to keep trouble away. The only man on earth with all his trouble behind him is a school bus driver!

There is no escape from trouble—not by fantasy, not by drugs or alcohol, not by psychotherapy. But having trouble does not mean that God has forgotten you. Nor does it imply that He does not love you. Trouble is living proof that you are a card-carrying member of the human race. King David wrote, "The Lord is my Shepherd . . . I will fear no evil." He did not say, "I will face no evil."

Trouble can be an asset! We often run from it and complain about it, but trouble helps to make us what we are. Our antagonist turns out to be our helper. It strengthens our muscles, sharpens our wits, and develops our skills. Trouble turns your spine into steel.

Trouble is resistance, and resistance is a key to progress. Without the resistance of air, a bird can't fly. Without the resistance of water, a ship can't float. Without the resistance of gravity, you can't walk. If you have no resistance, you will make little or no progress.

Dr. Marie Ray, a nationally known psychiatrist, studied the personalities of great men and women to see if there was a common denominator in their success. There was! The one thing they all had in common was trouble, in various forms. Dr. Ray's conclusion was this: No one succeeds in life who is not driven by trouble to be their very best.

Many significant people overcame great troubles. Glen Cunningham suffered burns on over ninety percent of his body in a schoolhouse fire. His doctors said, "You'll never walk again." But Glen not only walked again; he ran! In fact, he broke the world record in the one-mile run. Though blind and deaf, Helen Keller graduated from college with honors. Alexander the Great had epilepsy. Franklin Delano Roosevelt was elected president of the United States, while he was confined to a wheelchair by polio.

Our Savior also faced tremendous difficulties. He was called illegitimate in the streets of Nazareth. He was called a heretic by the recognized church. The state called him a traitor and an insurrectionist too dangerous to live. The Bible refers to Jesus as "a Man of sorrows and acquainted with grief" (Is. 53:3).

Do you know the difference between a priceless diamond and a common lump of coal? The diamond is a lump of coal that has endured intense pressure. The trouble it endured made it priceless. Saint Paul wrote in 2 Corinthians, "We are hard-pressed on every side, yet not crushed; we are perplexed, but not in despair; persecuted, but not forsaken; struck down, but not destroyed" (4:8–9).

One day, a fire broke out in the laboratory of Thomas Edison. The lab was destroyed, and all of Edison's experiments were lost. After the fire, he walked through the rubble and water-drenched wreckage. He found a little package tied tightly together, and in the center of the package was Edison's own photograph. The photograph was burned around the edges and sprinkled with water, yet undamaged. Edison took his pen and wrote under the photo, "It didn't touch me."

An olive will not yield its virgin oil until it is crushed. Delicious grapes cannot make new wine until they are crushed. Trouble is the womb of greatness. Saint Paul prayed to God three times for the "thorn in his flesh" to be removed, and God said "No!" Heaven's answer was, "My grace is sufficient for you."

George Whitefield preached with asthma. Smith Wigglesworth conducted great healing services with mighty miracles, and then went home and rolled on the floor in agony with kidney stones. Johnathan Edwards was so nearsighted that ink would smear on his nose as he read from his sermon notes, *Sinners in the Hands of an Angry God*.

Trouble is an asset! King David wrote, "Yea, though I walk through the valley of the shadow of death, I will fear no evil; for You are with me" (Ps. 23:4). Notice the words *shadow of death*. The shadow of a sword can't cut me. The shadow of a lion can't harm me. The shadow of a rattlesnake can't bite me. A shadow is harmless and powerless. Jesus Christ, the

Champion of Calvary, has so completely defeated death that when believers die, they simply pass through a harmless shadow. It's powerless and painless! You may die without your family or your friends at your bedside, but Jesus will be there. He owns the real estate on both sides of the "Jordan River" in your day of trouble.

God's Two-Minute Warning

To reject trouble is to reject the Word of God. Trouble is the messenger of God. The Bible says, "Do not think it strange concerning the fiery trial which is to try you" (1 Pet. 4:12). If you are angry at God for the trouble you are experiencing, recognize that because of His sovereign grace, God is allowing you to go through this time of trouble. His plan is to perfect His will in you. Don't resent trouble. It may well be the hand of God shaping you for His divine purpose.

CHAPTER NINETEEN

GOD'S TWO-MINUTE WARNING

MIRACLES COME IN CANS

The God of the Bible is a God of miracles!

On creation morning, God miraculously formed the heavens and the earth, separated light from darkness, and flung the glittering stars against the velvet of the night like glistening diamonds. He scooped a handful of dirt and breathed on it, and man became a living soul.

He divided the Red Sea for Moses and the children of Israel, enabling them to walk across on dry ground. He held the sun still for Joshua, while the enemies of Israel were defeated. He walked as the Fourth Man in the fiery furnace with the three Hebrew young men who refused to bow to the music and image of Nebuchadnezzar.

God the Father sent His Son to the Earth in the womb of a virgin, making Christmas a celebration of His miracle power. The Son, like the Father, had a ministry based on miracles. People didn't come by the thousands to hear Jesus just because of His teachings. They came to see the miracle power of God on parade.

Jesus healed the blind, the lame, and the lepers. He stopped a funeral procession, raised a dead boy back to life, and transformed the procession into a party. When He stood before the tomb of Lazarus and shouted, "Lazarus come forth," the man who had been dead for three days walked out of his tomb. Jesus had so much miracle power that if he had not specifically called Lazarus by name, every dead man on the face of the earth would have come out of his grave.

You may need a miracle today. If so, understand: God wants you to have your miracle more than you want the miracle!

Are miracles really for today? The answer is an emphatic "Yes!"

The Bible says, "Jesus Christ is the same yesterday, today and forever" (Heb. 13:8). That means what He did by the shores of Galilee in Israel, He can do in your life right now. All that Jesus is can be in you right this moment, by the power of His Holy Spirit.

One man said to me, "Pastor Hagee, I don't believe in miracles."

I replied, "You will, when you need one."

If miracles were supposed to cease with the apostles as some modern theologians teach, then why did James instruct believers to pray for miraculous healings? In James 5 we read, "Is anyone among you sick? Let him call for the elders of the church, and let them pray over him, anointing him with oil in the name of the Lord. And the prayer of the faith will save the sick" (14–15).

Keep in mind, James was the last apostle (though some might arguably wish to give that honor to the apostle Paul).

James didn't give the impression that miracles were to stop happening at the end of his lifetime or at the conclusion of any other spiritual leaders' lives. If God wanted miracles to stop, why did the Holy Spirit inspire the last apostle to teach the church to keep praying and believing for miracles in the future? Clearly, miracles are to be expected in our contemporary churches as well as in biblical days.

WHERE DO YOU FIND MIRACLES?

You find miracles in cans! When you start saying, "I can do all things through Christ who strengthens me," you are fostering the miracle mentality. Begin to say, "I can have a better marriage," "I can be free from the chains of alcohol and drug addiction," "I can be healed from this dreaded disease in my body," or "I can climb this impossible mountain." If you believe that you can, then with God's help, you will!

THREE BARRIERS TO YOUR MIRACLE

Three stumbling blocks often prevent believers from experiencing God' s miraculous power in their lives: fear, intellectual idolatry, and doubt.

1. **Fear.** The Scripture says, "For God has not given us a spirit of fear, but of power and of love and of a sound mind" (2 Tim. 1:7). The admonition Jesus used most frequently in His ministry was "Fear not." We are told not to fear poverty, for God will "supply all your need according to His riches in glory" (Phil. 4:19). We are told not to fear sickness for He is

the Great Physician. We are told not to fear death itself, for Jesus is the Resurrection and the Life! We are told not to fear the past, because the grace of God has buried it in the sea of forgetfulness, never to be remembered against us anymore. We are not to fear the future, because God is in the future, preparing it for us. I don't know what the future holds, but I know Who holds the future. Fear not!

2. **Intellectual Idolatry.** "Stubbornness is as iniquity and idolatry . . ." (1 Sam. 15:23). Stubborn people will not change their minds, even in the presence of truth as presented in God's Word. Why won't they change their minds? Because their thoughts and their opinions are more sacred to them than the Word of God. As long as they live in intellectual idolatry, they will never experience the miracles of God in their lives.

3. **Doubt.** The Bible continuously commands believers to "have faith in God." Doubt is like a cancer that destroys your faith in God. Rather than entertaining your doubts, feed your faith, and you will be pleasantly surprised at the miracles that take place as a result.

God's Two-Minute Warning

Romans 14:23 states, "But he who doubts is condemned . . . for whatever is not from faith is sin." And Revelation 21:8 states, "But the cowardly, unbelieving [doubters] . . . shall have their part in the lake which burns with fire and brimstone, which is the second death."

We need to see doubt as a major obstacle to our spiritual progress. In fact, God places doubters in the company of the most despicable people on earth! Doubting God is nothing more than practical atheism. Have faith in God because nothing is impossible to those who believe.

CHAPTER TWENTY

GOD'S TWO-MINUTE WARNING

SET AN EXAMPLE

Never in human history has it been more difficult to be a successful parent than today. The shelves of every bookstore are packed with advice on how to raise your children and be a successful parent. These books may be extremely helpful, but all of the books in the world combined cannot compare to the infinite wisdom contained in the Word of God.

Every parent must answer these important questions: Will you raise your children by the laws of Dr. Spock or the laws of God? Will you allow your precious sons and daughters to drown in the sewer of permissive, secular humanism, in which there is no absolute right or wrong, or will you teach your children to live on the Solid Rock, where every person is responsible for his or her own conduct, where choices have consequences, and you live or die by those choices? Every moment that you delay in raising your children according to God's Word, you are giving the opposition a clear, undefended shot at them.

The Lord told Moses to speak to the parents of Israel saying, "You must not do as they do in Egypt, where you used to live, and you must not do as they do in the land of Canaan, where I am bringing you. Do not follow their practices. You must obey my laws" (Lev. 18:3–4, NIV).

Peter writes, "But you are a chosen generation, a royal priesthood, a holy nation, His own special people [different from the world], that you may proclaim the praises of Him who called you out of darkness into His marvelous light" (1 Pet. 2:9). Christian families are not odd, but they are definitely different from the world—or at least they ought to be!

Paul recorded a revolutionary statement in Ephesians 6:4 when he said, "And you, fathers, do not provoke your children to wrath, but bring them up in the training and admonition of the Lord."

Notice that God placed the responsibility of spiritual training squarely on the shoulders of the father. Dads, getting the kids into church, Christian youth activities, and other opportunities for spiritual growth is not something you can shrug off and expect your wife to handle. Your children's spiritual growth is your responsibility too!

Paul's statement was especially revolutionary because there was a law in Rome called the Patria Potestes, meaning the Father's Power. The fathers of Rome had absolute power over their children. A father literally had the right to kill the child at birth, if he so desired. He could sell his children as slaves, or punish them with torture. When a child was born in Rome, he was laid at the feet of his father, and if the father picked the child up, the child lived. But the father turned his back on the child, the child was thrown into the streets. From there, the child could be taken to the forum where female babies would be picked up by Roman pimps who would raise the child for prostitution purposes. If the child was male, he could become a slave or a gladiator trained to fight and kill, just to amuse the aristocracy of Rome.

When Paul said, "Fathers provoke not your children to wrath," it was shocking to the people of his culture. The concept of a father receiving his child with tenderness and compassion was totally foreign to many of Paul's readers.

The Bible portrays children as a gift from God. Jesus said in Matthew 18:5, "Whoever receives one little child like this in My name receives Me." David wrote in Psalm 127:3, "Behold, children are a heritage from the Lord, the fruit of the womb is a reward. Like arrows in the hand of a warrior, so are the children of one's youth. Happy is the man who has his quiver full of them."

DO NOT PROVOKE YOUR CHILD

Scripture commands that we are to bring our children up in the discipline and instruction of the Lord instead of provoking them to anger. What does it mean to provoke a child to anger, and how can we avoid doing it? Here are some tips that will help:

➤You can provoke your child by being overly possessive. Deprive your child of expression, fence them in, and refuse them the opportunity of self-discovery, and they will be provoked. The older your child gets, the more freedom for self-discovery they need. When they leave your home as an adult, their skills of decision making should be in place. Otherwise, you release a lamb into a society of wolves.

➢You can provoke your child by preferring one child over another or comparing one child to another by saying, "Why can't you be like your older brother or younger sister?" Two of the most powerful businessmen I know carry deep emotional scars from parents who constantly compared them to their siblings in unfavorable ways.

Rebekah preferred Jacob over Esau. Isaac preferred Esau over Jacob. The preferential treatment of father and mother destroyed their family. Jacob and Esau hated each other most of their adult lives.

➢You can provoke your child by setting unrealistic, unattainable goals for them. After I graduated from Trinity University, I coached football for one year. One day, a father came to my office and described his son as a surefire, future all-American. By the way the dad talked, I expected to see a mammoth Adonis walk through my office door. When the boy entered my office, I was shocked. He would have had difficulty carrying the flute in the band! I dismissed the boy and lectured his father about unrealistic goals.

➢You can provoke your child by overindulging them. If you want to raise a certified brat, then just give your child what he wants, when he wants it.

➤ You can provoke your child with discouragement. Working without reward is destructive. A great Irish novel was written on the theme of the road to nowhere. During the Irish Depression, the government gave men jobs to build a road. It gave them a sense of purpose and dignity, and the work produced joy in the land. And then it was discovered that the road led to nowhere. It was work without purpose or reward. The news destroyed their joy and their initiative and turned their work into sheer drudgery. Don't worry; you won't spoil your children by giving them praise, encouragement, or rewards for a job well done.

➤ You can provoke your child by pretending to be perfect. It sounds like this, "When I was your age, blah . . . blah . . . blah!"

➤ You can provoke your child by neglect! According to a UCLA study, the average father in America spends just forty seconds a day talking to his children. That's neglect! One of the most common remarks I hear from children in our society is, "My daddy never has time to play with me."

➤ You can provoke your child with your toxic speech. Abusive words, criticism, and sarcasm will destroy your child emotionally, intellectually, and spiritually. Many fathers literally devastate their children with their hateful speech.

➤ You can provoke your child with physical abuse. No parent has a right to abuse a child. Physical discipline should always be administered when you are calm, and it should be done in love and self-control, not in vicious anger or retribution for something your child has said or done.

God's Two-Minute Warning

Matthew 18:5 gives a solemn warning to parents concerning their children: "Whoever receives one little child like this in My name receives Me. Whoever causes one of these little ones who believe in Me to sin, it will be better for him if a millstone were hung around his neck, and he were drowned in the depth of the sea." The parent who provokes a child provokes God!

How much better both parents and children will be when we nurture our children to godliness, by letting them see a loving example of Christ in us!

CHAPTER TWENTY-ONE

GOD'S TWO-MINUTE WARNING

WORRY IS A RAT

Do you have a Ph.D. in worry?

Do you worry more than you should?

Medical science confirms that worry is a serious contributing factor in the development of many major illnesses. Worry is like a rocking chair. It will give you something to do, but it won't get you anywhere. Worry can't change the past, but it can ruin the present.

We have a way out of worrying: we can take our problems and cares to the Lord in prayer. A problem not worth praying about is not worth worrying about. Worry means that there is something we cannot control, and if we are honest, it is something that causes us to feel irritated with God.

Jesus Christ made the most profound statements about worry that the world has ever heard. He said, "Therefore I say to you, do not worry about your life, what you will eat or what you will drink; nor about your body, what you will put on. . . . Which of you by worrying can add one cubit to his stature? . . . Therefore do not worry, saying, 'What shall we eat?' or 'What shall we drink?' or 'What shall we wear?' . . . Therefore do not worry about tomorrow, for tomorrow will worry about its own things." (Matt. 6:25, 27, 31, 34). Five times in this short passage of Scripture Jesus says, "Don't worry."

Have you ever noticed how worry tends to increase commensurately with the tension and pressure points in our lives? Worry often comes at a time of crisis. Just when you need a clear mind and steady nerves to make the wisest decision possible, here comes worry—like a dark cloud that obstructs the warmth and light of the sun. Worry drains you of your ability to think creatively and can cause many other problems.

➢Worry fills the face with wrinkles and apprehension. It robs the body of rest at night and sends you to work shattered, shaky, and second rate, living on the ragged edge.

➢Worry is the mother of cancer, heart disease, high blood pressure, ulcers, and a host of other diseases. Worry has sent millions of Bible-believing Christians to the cemetery long before their appointed time, men and women who knew the Prince of Peace! Worry is fear, rather than faith.

➢Worry is a predisposition toward defeat and despair. One old man said, "Most of the troubles I've worried about in life never happened."

HOW TO CONQUER WORRY

Never worry about things you can't change. The prayer of Saint Francis of Assisi captures this thought, "Lord grant me the courage to change the things I can, grace to bear what I can't change, and the wisdom to know the difference."

Don't worry about things you can change—just change them! Have you ever laid in bed, shivering on a cold winter night, with a blanket just six feet away? You didn't want to get up; you didn't want to move to get the blanket. It was less work to lie there and worry about being cold throughout the night. The solution to worry is to do something about it . . . or tell your spouse to get up and get the blanket!

Don't worry about your enemies for King David has written, "When the wicked came against me to eat up my flesh, my enemies and foes, they stumbled and fell, though an army may encamp against me, my heart shall not fear; though war may rise against me, in this will I be confident" (Ps. 27:2–3).

Don't worry about your fear, "For God has not given us a spirit of fear, but of power and of love and of a sound mind" (2 Tim. 1:7).

Don't worry when you feel overwhelmed by the pressures of life. The apostle Paul says, "Rejoice in the Lord always. Again I will say, rejoice!" (Phil. 4:4). King David said, "This is the day the Lord has made; we will rejoice and be glad in it" (Ps. 118:24). If you woke up this morning and didn't find your name in the obituary column, rejoice!

THREE REASONS NOT TO WORRY

1. **God is your Father, and He has the power to give you everything you need.** As a matter of fact, God took care of every need you ever had long before you knew you had a need! Before you were hungry, He gave the ground the ability to grow food. Before you were cold, He provided wool, wood,

and coal to help warm us. Before you were ever thirsty, He provided water for the nations of the world to drink.

2. **Worry produces absolutely nothing!** Jesus said, "Which of you by worrying can add one cubit to his stature?" The Greek word for stature is *elekia*, which means "span of life." In other words, which of you can lengthen your life by worrying? You can't, so why worry?

We take vitamins, read diet books, jog in the rain, and join health clubs as we try to lengthen our life. While a healthy lifestyle is part of good stewardship—taking proper care of the bodies God has given us—our lives are in the Lord's hands. The best pill, as one preacher put it, is the "Gos-pill." Jesus was the Great Physician and the Master Architect of the body, so you can trust the Owner's manual that He has given us. That manual states, "This machine is not designed to worry, since the Manufacturer has already taken care of every need you will ever have." That's better than a life insurance program; that's a life *assurance* program!

3. **Worry is a rat!** I read a story of an aviator who flew around the world. He stopped every few hours at selected landing fields to refuel. On one leg of his journey, two hours from his selected landing field and exactly halfway from his destination, he heard a noise in his plane that he recognized as the gnawing of a rat.

Not knowing which delicate indicators might be destroyed by the sharp teeth of the rat, the pilot began to worry. Then he remembered that rats are rodents and that they do not function well at heights. A rat is made to live on the ground and in dark holes. Consequently, the pilot pointed his plane higher and higher, until the gnawing stopped. Two hours later, when he landed safely, a dead rat fell out of the cockpit.

The way to kill off your worries is to take your life up a notch. Keep your eyes on Jesus, keep pressing onward and upward, trusting Him as you go higher and higher. As you focus on Christ, the "rats" that are trying to eat away at your peace and security will drop off one by one. Your worries will not survive.

God's Two-Minute Warning

Worry is the rejection of faith, and the rejection of faith turns godly Christians into practicing atheists. No wonder the Bible says, "Without faith it is impossible to please Him" (Heb. 11:6). We cannot worry and trust Him at the same time.

Worry is a rat that cannot live "in the secret place of the Most High." It cannot breathe in the atmosphere of faith and confidence. If your life's course has been altered by worry, then climb . . . climb . . . climb higher into the presence of the living God. Feel His peace and His reassuring touch. Experience His love and the joy of His presence. Worry must die in this divine atmosphere.